# The Music of Being

*of related interest*

**The Music in Music Therapy**
**Psychodynamic Music Therapy in Europe:**
**Clinical, Theoretical and Research Approaches**
*Edited by Jos De Backer and Julie P. Sutton*
*Foreword by Professor Paul Williams*
ISBN 978 1 84905 353 2
eISBN 978 0 85700 712 4

**Music Technology in Therapeutic**
**and Health Settings**
*Edited by Wendy L. Magee*
*Foreword by Dr David W. Ramsey*
ISBN 978 1 84905 273 3
eISBN 978 0 85700 570 0

**Early Childhood Music Therapy**
**and Autism Spectrum Disorders**
**Developing Potential in Young Children**
**and their Families**
*Edited by Petra Kern and Marcia Humpal*
*Foreword by David Aldridge*
ISBN 978 1 84905 241 2
eISBN 978 0 85700 485 7

**Music Therapy in Schools**
**Working with Children of All Ages**
**in Mainstream and Special Education**
*Edited by Jo Tomlinson, Philippa Derrington*
*and Amelia Oldfield*
*Foreword by Dr. Frankie Williams*
ISBN 978 1 84905 000 5
eISBN 978 0 85700 474 1

**Music Therapy with Children**
**and their Families**
*Edited by Amelia Oldfield*
*and Claire Flower*
*Foreword by Vince Hesketh*
ISBN 978 1 84310 581 7
eISBN 978 1 84642 801 2

# The Music of Being

Music Therapy, Winnicott and
the School of Object Relations

**Alison Levinge**

Jessica Kingsley *Publishers*
London and Philadelphia

Excerpt on p.15 from *The Practice of Psychoanalytic Parent-Infant Psychotherapy: Claiming the Baby*, Tessa Baradon, Carol Broughton, *et al.*, Copyright (2006) Routledge, reproduced by permission of Taylor & Francis Books UK. Excerpts from *Imprisoned Pain and Its Transformation: A Festschrift for H. Sydney Klein* by J. Symington on p.29 (2000) and from *The Maturational Processes and the Facilitating Environment* on p.55 (1990) are reprinted with kind permission of Karnac Books. Excerpt on p.75 from *Playing and Reality*, D.W. Winnicott, Copyright (2008) Routledge, reproduced by permission of Taylor & Francis Books UK. Excerpt on p.89 from *Babies and Their Mothers* (1988) is reprinted with kind permission of Free Association Books. Figs 6.1a and 6.1b on p.95, and Figs 6.2a and 6.2b on p.98 were originally published in *Through Paediatrics to Psychoanalysis: Collected Papers* by Donald W. Winnicott in 1975, and are reprinted with kind permission of Karnac Books. Excerpt on p.103 from *Deprivation and Delinquency*, D.W. Winnicott, Copyright (1984) Routledge; and excerpt on p.141 from *Introduction to Psychotherapy (2ed)*, D. Brown and J. Pedder, Copyright (1991) Routledge, reproduced by permission of Taylor & Francis Books UK.

Every effort has been made to trace copyright holders and to obtain their permission for the use of copyright material. The author and the publisher apologize for any omissions and would be grateful if notified of any acknowledgements that should be incorporated in future reprints or editions of this book.

First published in 2015
by Jessica Kingsley Publishers
73 Collier Street
London N1 9BE, UK
and
400 Market Street, Suite 400
Philadelphia, PA 19106, USA

*www.jkp.com*

Copyright © Alison Levinge 2015
Front cover image source: Shutterstock®.

**Library of Congress Cataloging in Publication Data**
Levinge, Alison.
The music of being : music therapy, Winnicott and the school of object relations / Alison Levinge.
pages cm
Includes bibliographical references and index.
ISBN 978-1-84905-576-5 (alk. paper)
1. Music therapy. 2. Object relations (Psychoanalysis) 3. Winnicott, D. W. (Donald Woods), 1896-1971.
I. Title.
ML3920.L47 2015
615.8'5154--dc23
2014036697

**British Library Cataloguing in Publication Data**
A CIP catalogue record for this book is available from the British Library

ISBN 978 1 84905 576 5
eISBN 978 1 78450 019 1

Printed and bound in the United States

# Contents

# Acknowledgements

This book has had a long gestation period which began with my meeting the psychoanalyst and author Adam Phillips in the context of a staff supervision group. Following an individual consultation, Adam became my external supervisor for my doctorate. Without his brilliance of insight, his ability to think outside the box in working with processes which occurred in a different medium than his own, this book would not be here. I particularly want to thank him for introducing me to Winnicott, both through elaborating his ideas in a highly thought-provoking way and providing me with what became my psychoanalytic bible, his own book *Winnicott*. Finally, I want to thank him for enabling me to play with my ideas without being frightened and for allowing me to believe that I have something to say.

I also need to thank Fiona Gardner, who has gently supported me in actually formulating my book and encouraged me to continue with the difficult final processes. One could say she has been the ideal midwife.

# Introduction

In a recent music therapy session with seven-year-old Andrea, and following our musical playing together, she initiated a discussion about her difficulties, or 'problems', as she named them. She was a bright, engaging and articulate little girl, who at this particular moment of our session found herself struggling as she tried to put her feelings into words. Suddenly, and sighing heavily, she looked up at me and exclaimed, 'It is like being in a tomato!' This vivid image, so beautifully word-painted by Andrea, captured for her a particular quality of her state of mind and through the directness of her image, allowed us to be able to think about what might be happening in her inner world of feelings.

In the music therapy room children and adults come to us in order to find some understanding and in the hope that something of what they bring can become transformed. Many of those who we see have no words and no symbolic language through which they can represent aspects of their inner feelings and thoughts. Others may have the use of language, yet may find they are unable to express themselves in ways that we can easily comprehend. As music therapists, we often find ourselves working with those who have difficulties in the area of communication. Discovering a means by which we can give shape and meaning to our patient's musical expressions that are lodged within 'that part of the psyche that lives in the wordless world' (Bollas 1991, p.3) can lead us to reach for various models of therapeutic practice. Illuminating the formless and perhaps chaotic elements of our patients' lives is required, if they are to feel understood and, as a way of resolving this dilemma, music therapists may have found themselves borrowing from other sources of psychological thinking.

As a music therapy practitioner who acknowledges the unconscious as well as conscious processes of a therapeutic relationship, I have turned to considering what psychoanalysts have termed the primitive state of mind – or as Winnicott described, 'primitive types of object relations' (1992, p.146) – and which by its nature, is present at a time 'before the infant knows himself (and therefore others) as the whole person that he is (and that they are)' (p.149). Winnicott and some of those following in his footsteps have described that working with patients who are severely psychologically disturbed can teach you more about what it means to be alive, or as Pedder in his foreword suggests, can help us to 'get to the very root of selfhood' (Abram 1996, p.xix). Bollas writes how therapy with an autistic child taught him 'how to attend to this wordless element in an adult' (1991, p.3) and working in this world of wordlessness is central to our practice.

As music therapists, the means by which we try and engage with our patients is through the creative and non-verbal medium of music. We do this by presenting the children or adults whom we see with an array of small and large percussion instruments that come from different cultures. These attractive objects can easily be made to create varied and interesting sounds, requiring no musical skill. In our role as therapists and through our musical training we utilise our musicianship to resonate with, connect to and reflect all the different musical expressions and gestures our patients may make. Usually, we do this through the technique named clinical improvisation, which, as a free form of music-making, allows us to remain in the musical moment, moving with the pace of the child or adult's communications.

Working with a primarily non-verbal language that can access primitive states of being may be both challenging and rewarding. The fact that as music therapists we have a means by which we can enter the frightening and confusing world of a child or adult, is a gift. But I have come to believe that if I am to help a patient to find some relief and transformational quality to their life, then it is not enough that I create a space in which I can be with them. I consider that in order that my own capacity to remain connected to external reality is sustained and that a child or adult in the room can discover a pathway toward a more integrated state of being, it is necessary for me to find the means by which some sense of what has happened between us can be made. Being in a therapeutic relationship, reading and thinking about pre-verbal states of mind has brought me to a form of understanding that has not just connected to my cognitive processes alone. As Bollas has suggested, studying the early states of being can enable us to reach a much earlier and wordless place, one in which we begin our lives. To find the words to explain or describe the feelings which emanate from being in contact with this pre-verbal state can, as Andrea described, feel like being in a tomato!

At the beginning of my own professional life, and in search of a means by which I could make sense of the various music therapy encounters, I found myself led to consider the ideas of the paediatrician and psychoanalyst Donald Winnicott. His clinical work with over 60,000 families and their children provided him with rich material for his theory of human development and in particular for understanding pre-verbal states of being. His ideas have been recorded in various mediums such as papers, talks, books and broadcasts, but always in ways which have made even the most complex of ideas accessible.

A chance encounter with the psychoanalyst Adam Phillips led me to study Winnicott's writings and one could say that it was love at first read. So it is no surprise, therefore, that the man Winnicott and his ideas fill the heart of this book, for which I make no apology. However, in throwing my bonnet into the Winnicott ring, I am aware of a tendency to idealise this man along with his thinking. Clearly he was a charismatic figure as well as a gifted communicator, two characteristics which drew me into believing in a Winnicottian baby. But it is the lively and free style of his language along with the straightforwardness of the terms he uses to describe his ideas that make reading about his theory of human development so uplifting and illuminating. These qualities of Winnicott's writings, coupled with his playfulness and surprising turns of phrase, have brought me into a space in which, with a wave of his hand, so to speak, I have found myself able to think.

Since Winnicott died in 1971 there have been many advances in the understanding of infant behaviour. So much so, that the years beginning in the early 1990s have become known as the 'decade of the brain' (Schore 2001, p.27). Neurobiological discoveries have advanced, supporting our understanding of the importance of the early mother–baby relationship. And, in referring to this time, as Gerhardt tells us, 'We have arrived at a moment in which different disciplines are converging to produce a new understanding of emotional life' (2004, p.1). Gerhardt suggests that this has occurred not because of one particular breakthrough, but because of many things happening at once and through communication between such disciplines as 'neuroscience, psychology, psychoanalysis, and biochemistry'. This concept of a melting pot of ideas I believe connects to the integrity of Winnicott's ability to remain free in his thinking, whilst being wary of any dogmatism which may creep in to limit his understanding. So that far from diminishing his work and that of the early object relation theorists, recent discoveries have enhanced original developmental theories. And, as an ardent communicator, I cannot help but feel that Winnicott in particular would approve of the joining together of the different ways in which our understanding of what it means to be human has continued to evolve. After all, the relational elements of early life were at the core of his thinking and practice and continue to inform the work of therapists today.

Arising out of his lifelong study of the mother–baby relationship or, as Phillips tells us, 'what went on between the mother and her infant', Winnicott was provided with a source for his 'most striking and characteristic insights' (1988, p.6). Linking his earlier paediatric training with his later understanding 'derived from psychoanalysis' prompted Winnicott to form a belief that a child has a 'primary wish to be understood' (p.51) and that, by creating a psychoanalytic setting reflective of significant aspects of the early mother–infant relationship, allowed a 'metaphorical blackboard on which the patient chalks up his own observations' (p.54) to be created. His detailed study of early life enabled Winnicott to formulate a unique and lasting theory of human development, which in his determination and passionate drive to communicate with as wide an audience as possible, was in essence, as Abram tells us, delivered with a 'freedom of expression' (p.2).

Simple though his ideas might appear at times, they are actually complex and rich in perception, and have provided me with a fertile and rewarding soil into which I have planted my own. Analysing and reflecting upon certain of Winnicott's concepts is at the heart of this book. My study has informed my own thinking, and an understanding of their relevance to music therapy practice has enabled me to formulate a particular theory of music therapy.

By interweaving my chosen theories of Winnicott with my own experiences in a music therapy setting, it has been my intention to shine a light upon the workings of a music therapy relationship. But as suggested by Davis and Wallbridge in introducing Winnicott, I would also like to request that 'the reader is invited to respond not with the intellect alone but with the whole self' (Davis and Wallbridge 1981, p.xi).

Following this introduction, the book continues in Chapter 1 by providing a background to the ideas and thinking of those who became central to the development of the school of object relations. I have chosen to frame my discussion within a general understanding of family dynamics and examine how the various members have influenced the organisation's overall development. I introduce the reader to some of the key figures in the movement and provide a brief overview of their significant theoretical contributions.

In the second chapter, two main aspects of Winnicott's life are explored. Initially, the reader is provided with a flavour of Winnicott's early years and how certain elements, which included a strong female presence, influenced his professional developmental. Music held a central role in Winnicott's life and, as a creative medium, I shall be exploring how this art form relates to his ability to communicate and look at the ways in which I see it has impacted upon his writing. I will consider how his love of music influenced his constant preoccupation with words and conclude with clinical examples introducing the reader to James and Katy.

In Chapter 3 I consider the power of music and how it can transform lives. I will examine its elements and look at how it exists in our lives even before we are born. I will introduce Joanne, a young adult with anorexia, and Jack, an elderly man with dementia, and discuss how music has helped to transform their lives.

In Chapters 4, 5, 6, 7, 8 and 9 I take specific concepts of Winnicott's and consider in what ways they may be used to clarify music therapy processes. Chapter 4 looks at Winnicott's concept of holding, which he uses to describe an essential element of the first environment. I refer to Bowlby's ideas on early attachment and briefly explain the differences in their understanding of an infant's

*Summary of chapters*

beginnings. The focus then moves to music therapy with Daniela, in which I consider in what ways music may be used to hold a child or adult in music therapy.

Chapter 5 is the first of four in which I consider Winnicott's specialised understanding of play. I begin by discussing his observations of the first moments in which a mother with her baby are invited to meet with him in his consultation setting. We will meet David, Olivia and Max, who in music therapy show in what ways one of the most significant elements of this process, that is, the 'period of hesitation', can reveal aspects of the internal world of a child or adult's difficulties.

In Chapter 6 I take one of the most important of Winnicott's ideas and one which has contributed most to early developmental theory. That is his concept of transitional objects and transitional phenomena. This introduces the reader to what Winnicott names as being 'the first not me possession' and looks at how this enables a baby to move from total dependence to a more separate and relative independent way of living. We meet Callum, who finds separation difficult to manage but is clearly grappling with this stage of his development. We encounter Tim, who finds his own pathway toward a place in which we could both play together and Peter, who continues to struggle with finding a way of being in a world that is external to that of his own creation.

Chapter 7 is divided into two parts and discusses what could be considered the less popular concepts of aggression and hate. In the first part I look at Winnicott's use of the word 'aggression', exploring its significance in an infant's development of being able to relate and use objects. In the second part we move on to the more sophisticated form that Winnicott names 'hate', considering its part in a mother's response to her baby, and its role in developing a capacity for concern. The chapter concludes by examining the importance of the unconscious destructive drive in enabling an infant to discover a capacity to find and use the object. We meet Kim, who appears paralysed by her unprocessed aggression toward the original object and Jake who, in part, teaches me the meaning of what it is to survive as a music therapist. Finally, we are introduced to Becky, whose destructiveness became expressed covertly, resulting in a meaningless quality to our exchanges.

Chapter 8 introduces the reader to Winnicott's well-known concept of play. We learn how being playful was a central aspect of Winnicott's personality and central to his practice. His theory of play is defined, and as a way of exploring the idea of musical play, the reader is initially introduced to Susan, who is autistic, and Simon, who has a diagnosis of schizophrenia.

Chapter 9 considers one of Winnicott's most unique ideas, and one that he names as being a 'sense of self'. We visit the music therapy room once more in order to see how this simple yet puzzling concept plays out.

Leading into consideration of therapeutic practice, Chapter 10 begins by introducing the reader to the psychoanalytic tools of transference and countertransference. As therapists we need to become aware of how the information we receive about our patients can be delivered both consciously and unconsciously and that, if we are to work with a patient's inner world, these two phenomena are most helpful.

The book concludes by providing a brief discussion on therapeutic technique and in Chapter 11 considers the overall stance that we need to take as therapists in order that we can be of most use to the children and adults with whom we work.

In relation to specific terminology, throughout the book I will be using the male pronoun 'he'. But before I continue, I need to explain to the reader that I have had always had difficulty with the politically correct term *client* as used to describe a child or adult who comes for therapy. It seems to me that this word has been borrowed from a more legalistic culture and therefore, for me, creates a rather distant objective quality to what is a profoundly intimate relationship. There does not appear to be a suitable different label; therefore, with the reader's forbearance I have chosen to use the term 'patient' throughout the book, a term adopted by early psychoanalysts.

# CHAPTER 1

# Object Relations

*Past experiences give complex meaning to the present*
(Baradon *et al.* 2006, p.12)

As social animals, human lives involve the making and sometimes breaking of relationships. This begins when we enter the world, and into a social system formed by our immediate family members. In our family of origin, patterns of relating are woven one with another and, as expressed in the initial quote, for new parents, this includes the connection to past experiences of attachment. Caring for a new baby will evoke in a mother and father feelings related to their own early infant–parent relationship. If there were difficulties in attachment which remain unresolved, these may then become represented in their current mode of parental care. As part of therapeutic practice, it is important to be able to gain a sense of the early model of attachment and a formal interview in which a patient's story can be heard is one way in which this can be achieved. Significant material about relationships and their representations may be gathered from an initial structured interview with either the family or the patient themselves. Equally, and in a more freely associative way, a moment to moment monitoring of the interview process by a therapist can also provide valuable information and, along with the more formalised history taking, support the forthcoming therapeutic process.

## Shelley

Shelley was referred for music therapy when she was three. In the initial interview several disturbing and significant factors emerged that helped to throw light on Shelly's current difficulties. Her mother described that at certain times and, whenever she found herself in an enclosed space, Shelley would fall into a desperate state of terror. Following her 'release', Shelley would remain quite listless, curling up in a ball and sucking her thumb until such time as she felt able to come back to life, so to speak. Mother also reported that if ever she was about to leave Shelley, if only for a short while, her daugthter would become very clingy, holding onto her as if her life depended upon it. When we came to discuss her pregnancy, Mother looked at me directly and, with a quality of desperate sadness, announced that she had never wanted children. As Mother's story unfolded, she revealed her deep ambivalence toward Shelley, her only child, explaining that she had been conceived during a one-night stand. Finding it was too late for an abortion, she had begun to feel that she was some kind of monster, and worried that she would give birth to a deformed baby.

Enquiring further, Mother relayed the dreadfulness of the delivery and how, once in labour, it was discovered that Shelley was very large and as a result she had become stuck in the birth canal. An emergency Caesarean was performed, but for some reason the anaesthetic failed. Mother's dreadful physical pain became intensified by her visual experience of the blood and mess accompanying the operation, and following the birth process, she became severely depressed. Mother described that from the beginning, Shelley appeared to be an anxious baby. She would desperately seek physical contact, but almost simultaneously appear to reject it. The vividness of Mother's description created an image of a tortured-like state in which Shelley and mother found themselves living. As we concluded our discussion, Mother continued by telling me that as she was being fed, Shelly would hold onto the teat of her bottle with a fierce strength, but then almost immediately try to spit it out, as if it was disgusting.

Shelley's behaviour in the therapy room appeared to be a re-enactment of her own and her mother's early traumas. At one moment in a session, Shelley would become overwhelmed by persecutory feelings, and would struggle to remain in the room. In the next, she would be curled up underneath the piano, terrified to move. Shelley's painful and distressing behaviour appeared to reflect something of her birth experience, which had been so traumatic, as well as aspects of the deeply ambivalent nature of her mother's feelings toward her. Mother's deep distress and

Shelley's overwhelming sense of abandonment were reconfirmed when in a later meeting she described that following Shelley's delivery she had even feared to look at her new baby.

Over the months of therapy and with gentle containment and thoughtfulness on my part, Shelley's terror began to diminish. As she felt safer, Shelley was able to discover a psychic space in which to begin to think about how awful she felt. Rather than enact her feelings, Shelley started to find the words that could define something of the horror of her internal world.

Patterns of relationship also occur within organisations and the dynamics which develop can be viewed as representing similar processes to those which occur within a family. In the follwing discussion I will be reflecting upon the birth of the school of object relations and, in my brief reflections on its historical background, hope to bring a certain understanding of two of its most influential theorists, that is Donald Winnicott and John Bowlby. Due to the nature of the material however, the following part of this chapter is more factual in style. But it is hoped that the history of this psychoanalytic family will provide the reader with the context in which these two figures emerged. As Winnicott's ideas are central to this book, and in order to acknowledge the significance of his contributions, I end the chapter with a short history of the psychoanalyst John Bowlby. His ideas were initially received with mixed feelings by the British School of Psychoanalysts. Yet his thinking about early attachment relationships continues to form a significant element of current work with disturbed children.

The school of object relations was initially a British development and grew out of the classical tradition of analysis begun by Freud. Its core belief was, as it says on the tin, an understanding of how we make contact with an object. In other words, it was a relational model of thinking rather than a biological one. As the 'father' of psychoanalysis, Freud's concept of human development proffered a model of growth in which psychology was, at its root, a physical matter. He believed that as humans we are driven by biological drives and that the id, as it came to be named, and its drives are responsible for 'all that is most powerful in us' (Gomez 1998, p.14). As the object relations family developed its ideas and took on new members, its function and dynamics began to change. Unlike Freud, whose focus was on 'the adult's struggle with incompatible and unacceptable desires' (Phillips 1988, p.4), the new family of object relations theorists believed that from our beginnings we are in fact 'object seeking'. They considered that, from the commencement of our lives, we are propelled to seek out an other, and that as humans, we yearn for relationships. In fact it is our capacity for making relationships that makes us human.

The two words, 'object' and 'relations', that form the title adopted by this psychoanalytic family, appear at odds with each other. On the one hand the second term describes a relational aspect of life and on the other the term 'object' paints a picture of something detached and unconnected in quality. In common parlance the word 'object' tends to refer to inanimate aspects of life, such as a table, a chair etc. In the world of psychoanalysis, however, this term has come to represent a relational aspect of humanness, both conscious and unconscious, and is one which makes distinct our connections with the other, subject from object, object from subject. Studying the relationships of a person with his objects leads to the understanding that 'internal objects are viewed as reflections of experiences with real persons' (Gomez 1998, p.xii). The term 'object' can equally be used to refer to an aspect of the other, such as a body part for example, a mother's breast, or a function, such as being a doctor. In the latter case the object will be known as a 'part object'.

Reflecting upon the overall organisation of psychoanalysts, and as in every family, particular dynamics occur between its members on a daily basis. Ultimately these processes affect both how each individual within the system functions as well as the system as a whole, influencing its eventual development and that of the individuals within. In therapeutic practice, taking a family history includes gaining knowledge of how the family functions and in particular, the perspective taken by the parents. In the case of the object relations family, and in its early stages of becoming an established school of thinking, its beginnings arose out of Freudian thinking. Freudian theory brought to the then established psychoanalytic family an understanding of the human mind as being something that was physiologically rooted, considering it as being a concrete and assessable element. Reflecting a more formal and medicalised way of understanding human development, Freudian practice became known as 'classical' or 'traditional' psychoanalysis.

Taking a family history includes gaining knowledge of how the family functions and in particular, the perspective taken by the parents. Born an Austrian Jew, Freud, the 'father' of this particular family, began developing his unique understanding of the human psyche at a time in world history when conflict and turmoil were sending political and economic shudders throughout Europe. His cultural family were disintegrating. Therefore it is perhaps not surprising that Freud's primary understanding of human nature was one that saw human beings as embroiled in an inner conflict between forces for good and forces which are destructive. This wider family ambience created the backcloth to Freud's personal family culture which, by contrast, he was considered to be at 'the centre of attention'. So that whilst in the wider Jewish family persecution and oppression was growing and antagonistic attitudes were becoming an increasing force within his own family system, perhaps we could imagine that he could do no wrong. This intense difference between the two family cultures was perhaps the influence that created the catalyst that provoked Freud to develop his dualistic approach to his understanding of humanity. However, in the latter part of his life, his theories became more flexible and included reference to the significance of relationships in psychological development. Nevertheless, the predominant focus of Freud's theories was based upon his belief in a human being's constant state of conflict and that inside every human were the unconscious forces of life and death by which Freud believed we were driven.

When Freud arrived in London he was fleeing the violent regime which had now become established and, unbeknownst to him, he was entering the last year of his life. His establishment in the psychoanalytic family came 11 years after that of one whom we could imagine as being the 'mother figure'. Her name was Melanie Klein and, like her 'psychoanalytic partner', she too had immigrated to London. Klein was of Polish–Hungarian Jewish origin. Her relationship with Freud, however, was not straightforward and, along with her own early family difficulties, did not make her time in the psychoanalytic family easy. Klein had studied Freud's thinking, but she chose to take quite a different stance and one which became formative in establishing the movement of object relations. Suggesting the delicate nature of their relationship, and perhaps providing us with a hint of things to come, Klein made clear that her ideas were a development of Freud's thinking and not, as he himself described, a 'deviation'. The music of Freud's term is quite different and perhaps rather provocative in nature to that used by Klein, giving us some sense of the dynamics evolving in this 'mother–father' relationship. In contrast to the central element of Freud's thinking, Klein emphasised the importance of the inner world, and its interaction between the outside and external life of the human psyche. Klein's underlining of the therapist's need to listen to a patient's experiences emphasised the relational element of her theory, which was 'a theory of "subject relations"' (Gomez 1998, p.34). As already mentioned it is, as Gomez suggests, Klein's particular understanding of the human condition that pushes on the development of the object relations school of thinking and, interestingly, toward an ultimate divide between its family members.

Like Freud, Klein began her early professional pathway by planning to study medicine. Unlike Freud however, this plan became thwarted, thus setting her on a very different and definitely non-scientific psychoanalytic journey. Following a depression and a subsequent analysis, Klein was led into the world of psychoanalytic practice in which she eventually became qualified, and worked in the underdeveloped practice of child analysis. Perhaps one could view this development as reflecting as well as emphasising her mother role in this family. Klein's professional beginnings strongly influenced how her theoretical ideas developed, and we learn that her direct psychoanalytical experiences created a timbre of creativity and 'intuitively-driven interpretations of the most primitive layers of life' (Gomez 1978, p.31). Working with children provided her with the basis of her theories, which took on a subjective rather than objective stance. Klein believed that it was our 'hopes, fears and wishes experienced in bodily terms' (Gomez 1978, p.34) which formed our life force, rather than the 'instinctual drives' of Freud's theory.

Reflecting on Klein's immediate family culture, one could see that perhaps it was her own unhappy childhood that had propelled her into working with children. In her personal family system Klein is portrayed as being quite a sad and confused figure. Parented by a mother who confessed that her daughter was not a planned baby and a father who clearly preferred her sister, Klein's family environment was, as Grosskurth (1986) describes, entangled and neurotic. At the centre of the family dynamic was Klein's mother, a powerful and controlling figure, perhaps a characteristic that Klein inherited and one which evoked powerful responses within the professional family. Her personal experiences as a mother appeared in contrast to her stance as a therapist with children, which as we know is often the case in the world of therapy. In her newly found role as a parent, Klein became overwhelmed and sank into depression. We can hear the pain and agony in Klein's description of this time of her life as she writes, 'I knew all the time I was not happy, but saw no way out' (Grosskurth 1986, p.30).

Klein's struggles with her own mother, along with what appears to be quite an unappreciated place in the immediate psychoanalytic family, did not only contribute toward Klein's sibling rivalry with Anna Freud, but was in some part also a factor which brought about the ultimate theoretical divide that eventually arose within the psychoanalytic schools of thinking. Yet in spite of all these difficulties and perhaps because of her battles within both her personal and professional family life, Klein was led into becoming a significant influence in the development of child analysis. Arising from her own internal and external conflicts Klein provided us with a theory about the 'very primitive elements of the human mind' (Hinshelwood 1991, p.1). And as Gomez suggests, one which has helped us to 'bear the most dreadful parts of human beings' (Gomez 1978, p.53).

It is perhaps important at this point to mention the psychoanalyst Ronald Fairbairn. For although he is the least well known of the object relations family, he is acknowledged as being the first person to set out a full object relations theory of the personality. In describing him, I am tempted to repeat the cliché that it is 'always the quiet ones' when describing him, as this phrase is often used to depict the influence or power a less verbose and more hidden personality can have within a family system. Fairbairn was in character a quiet and retiring man and did not present himself in ways which would make him a high profile member. In part this was because of his geographical location, which was far away from London and situated in Edinburgh. One could say he was literally outside the family. But more significantly, it was due to Fairbairn's 'introspective' and retiring nature, which kept him working up to ten hours a day and writing until retiring to bed. These factors, plus his challenges to the tradition of psychoanalysis, 'all contributed to his marginalisation' (Gomez 1978, p.54). Yet Fairbairn contributed one of the most significant and influential ideas in psychoanalysis and one which remains today. In the classical tradition of analysis it was believed that it was the analytic technique rather than the relationship which enabled it to be effective. Interpretation was central to the therapeutic process, and it was considered that it was this therapeutic tool which enabled a patient to become aware of their hidden 'impulses' and perceptions. Challenging this practice, Fairbairn put forth the idea that it was the relationship between a therapist and patient that was the 'single most important factor in helping the patient to change' (Gomez 1978, p.74) and that this particular kind of relationship was more important than a 'proper' interpretation. Winnicott later underlines this element of object relations when in his description of psychoanalysis he writes: 'Psychoanalysis is not just a matter of interpreting the repressed unconscious, it is rather the provision of a professional setting for trust, in which such work may take place' (Winnicott 1986, p.115).

As well as challenging some of the psychoanalytic family's fundamental ideas, Fairbairn endorsed Klein's belief that it is in the first year of life that significant developments of an infant's personality take place and considered that object seeking behaviour begins at birth. Yet despite the fact that Fairbairn was neither a prolific writer nor a natural communicator and the fact that that there were many puzzling aspects to some of his theories, nevertheless, one of his biggest contributions to the object relations family was to effect a change in the attitude of psychoanalysts to their relationship with their patients. Equally, by revising Freud's model of the mind by proposing that infants were not as Freud suggested, seeking satisfaction through a biological drive, Fairbairn pushed the thinking of the movement away from the classical tradition. For the post-Freudian baby, the satisfaction of the baby came and still continues to do so in current thinking, through relationships with others.

Returning to the immediate object family, we now come to examine the siblings in this psychoanalytic family and are immediately introduced to Freud's daughter Anna, a potential rival

Origin
story   cont'd

of Klein. Although it was Freudian theory which gave the school of
object relations its start in life, with Freud's actual arrival in London,
along with his daughter Anna, an intensification of the theoretical
divide within the psychoanalytic family arose, and elements of
individual family backgrounds were evoked. Anna, who like Klein
was a child analyst, approached her practice differently and, in an
attempt to separate herself from Freud's daughter, prompted Klein to
remark that 'I'm a Freudian, but not an Anna Freudian' (Grosskurth
1986, pp.455–456). Klein in particular had felt ignored by her own
father and both Anna and Klein had fathers who had preferred their
sisters. Anna and Klein's obvious theoretical differences and conflict
of loyalties appeared to contribute to the eventual appearance of
cracks within the object relations family group. As a result, members
of the family were driven into separate camps, declaring their
allegiance to either the traditionalists and followers of Freud or to
those who aligned themselves with Klein, and who became known
as Kleinians. In terms of the family dynamic, one could say that
the rift between father and mother had finally begun to divide the
psychoanalytic family.

In an attempt to hold the British School of Psychoanalysts
together, certain analysts, of whom Winnicott was eventually one,
came to the rescue, helping to create what came to be named as the
Middle Group. Those who placed themselves within this group were
thinkers who were strongly associated with the psychotherapeutic
tool of countertransference and chose to believe that the origin of
certain psychopathologies was rooted in real external experiences.
Eventually, and perhaps as a way of acknowledging their
separateness from the original family, they came to name themselves
the Independent Group, or as some described them, the Group of
Independent Thinkers.

Describing Winnicott as a 'natural peace-maker' and perhaps
making a link to his later idea on the meaning of a third space
between mother and baby, Padel tells us that it was Winnicott who
did 'more than anybody else to keep the British Society together and,
at a time in the 1950s, when antagonisms between the followers of
Anna Freud and those of Melanie Klein were still most bitter' (Padel
2001, p.269). Winnicott's eventual position in the middle school
follows the arrival of the psychiatrist and psychoanalyst John Bowlby,

*Bowlby time*

whose name is synonymous with what continues to be known as attachment theory. Winnicott and Bowlby, as Issroff states, 'were perhaps the two most influential pioneering British child psychiatrists and psychoanalysts of the past century' (Issroff 2005, p.115). They both believed that an infant comes into the world 'predisposed to participating in social interaction' (p.115) and realised the damaging effects neglect, deprivation and inadequate parenting may have upon a child. Each emphasised the necessity for continuity of care and, in expressing this idea through their own particular style of thinking, promoted a way of understanding development which had at its centre an emphasis on health. But it is with Bowlby that I end this particular chapter.

Bowlby's practice in child psychiatry consolidated his belief that real experiences of interpersonal life are the origin of psychopathology. His understanding of the specific ways in which we make relationships enabled him to see that there were also a variety of ways in which we connect to, or, in the term used in his theory, attach to our first object. How we do this ultimately affects later relationships we make. Bowlby saw that separation and loss were two of life's processes which could cause the most disturbance if handled in a distressing way, and his early experiences as a psychiatrist cemented his belief in the impact of family interactions and what he came to understand as being 'intergenerational phenomena' (Issroff 2005, p.19). Bowlby turned to scientific developments to support the formulation of his ideas and unlike Winnicott, was more concerned with 'measurement and validation' than 'appreciation of the inner life of imagination …and the importance and richness of interplay of inner and outer worlds' (Issroff 2005, p.150). He was 'a nuts-and-bolts man' and 'liked hard data and researchable concepts' (Karen 1994, p.110). In his everyday life, Marrone (1998, p.15) describes Bowlby as being 'not very expressive', creating an impression of a rather reserved man. Given his family culture, we could imagine that this particular characteristic arose from the atmosphere within which he grew up, which was headed by parents who have been described as being 'aloof, with little capacity to express affection' (Marrone 1998, p.16). The picture painted of his early life is one that appears to reflect qualities associated with deprivation and is endorsed by the fact that at the tender age of seven Bowlby was sent to boarding school. One wonders how it is that there appeared be so little apparent effect of this rather austere upbringing. Gomez describes Bowlby as being an 'intriguing mixture of pompousness and sensitivity' and someone who was 'more at home with procedures than patients' (Gomez 1978, p.153).

His time at Cambridge as a student was spent reading natural sciences and psychology, which appears to have influenced his subsequent choice of study, developmental psychology. Following his graduation Bowlby spent time in a school for maladjusted children where he was led to realise the impact early family dysfunctional life could have upon the psychological development of children. He came to understand that early disturbed family relationships often caused a 'pathogenic effect on personality development' (Marrone 1998, p.16). And it was Bowlby's realisation that these real early external experiences of children's relationships with others were those which eventually become internally represented, affecting the ways in which a child continued to make other relationships. This led to his eventual development of what we now name as attachment theory.

Following his move to London, where he pursued his medical career, Bowlby began a psychoanalytic training. Klein became his supervisor, yet as Parkes comments, 'from the outset he seems to have found it hard to accept the dogmatic beliefs of his supervisors' (1995, p.250).

Bowlby's difficulty in agreeing with certain beliefs of the Kleinian school of thinking was confirmed when, having seen several depressed patients who had recently been bereaved, he realised the significance of external factors upon the development of their illness. Rather than basing ill health upon unconscious phantasies alone, Bowlby took into account the influence a patient's outside world could have upon the origin of their psychopathology.

This realisation was pivotal in his ultimate separation from the dogma of Kleinian thinking as well as from Klein herself. For Bowlby, 'the object of study of psychoanalysis was not the intrapsychic life of the individual in isolation but the psychological life of the individual in an interpersonal or social context' (Marrone 1998, p.21).

Bowlby's later membership of an annual discussion group formed in order to discuss the impact of inconsistencies in child care included the psychologist Piaget, whose influence allowed him to widen his

*Bowlby story origin cont'd*

thinking by introducing him to the study of ethology. This enabled Bowlby to revise his thinking on instinct theory and develop what became known as the internal working model of relationships.

Up until the mid-1950s, there was only one view 'of the nature and origin of affectional bonds' (Marrone 1998, p.24) held amongst psychoanalysts, and it was thought that attachment developed in order to reduce instinctual tension, for example when feeling hungry. Bowlby, on the other hand, and influenced by his wider studies of the natural world, saw that attachment was more likely to be linked to a child's need to survive and remained independent from the Kleinian and Freudian assumptions that attachment was a by-product of the feeding activity. In contrast, Bowlby's thesis identified five responses an infant makes toward its carer and he believed it was these that contributed to the means by which his attachment evolved. He labelled them as sucking, clinging, following, crying, and smiling and considered that they were 'specific to Man'. Bowlby's interest in the study of animal behaviour patterns began to raise concern amongst members of the psychoanalytic fraternity and, for the followers of Klein, was felt to be deviant. For others Bowlby's ideas were to be ignored.

Bowlby believed that current understanding of early development was concerned more with 'meaning and imagination' than by becoming a 'body of validated knowledge'. Leaning more toward a philosophical view of life, Bowlby perceived that the majority of psychoanalytic thinking presented as being non-scientific, and that this resulted in a failure to recognise 'the necessity to continually revise theory in the light of new discoveries' (Marrone 1998, p.154). During his time as head of the Department for Children and Parents Bowlby committed his work to research. His findings confirmed his belief that it was a continuity of maternal care that underpinned the healthy psychological development of children. His findings were supported further by the work of the Robertsons, who carried out detailed observations of young children and filmed their work. The results of their research, recorded in 1989, 'provided clear evidence that experiences of separation between a young child and his mother set in motion a sequence of psychological reactions which are likely to have long-term effects' (Marrone 1998, p.22).

Bowlby's connection with Winnicott was made during his time as Deputy President of the British Psychoanalytical Society between 1956 and 1961, during which time Bowlby established the Department for Children and Parents and child psychotherapy training, along with Esther Bick. Bowlby remained at the Tavistock until 1972 and, although he maintained an aspect of his clinical practice, during the 1960s he began to spend more time developing and writing up his ideas. It took him 15 years to write his trilogy entitled *Attachment and Loss*, for which he has become known. His books include ideas gathered from over his 30-year period of research and practice and some of them became used to inform social policies on child care. His focus upon his writing, coupled with the indifference and hostility he experienced from those within the British Psychoanalytical Society eventually drove Bowlby to withdraw. But, despite fundamental differences, Bowlby remained, one could say, attached to the Tavistock Clinic and his eightieth year was celebrated by those at the Tavistock Clinic with an international conference.

Bowlby's ideas continue to remain central to the thinking about early attachment and have provided practitioners working with children, in particular, with an effective method of understanding about the type of bond we may form in our early years. In developing his theory, Bowlby's ideas were based upon traditional psychoanalytic thinking, and his inclusion of developmental psychology along with the particular language he adopted to explain his view of early human life, remains as his signature.

To conclude, object relations theory rests upon the belief that 'the human being is essentially social: and "our need for contact is primary"' (Gomez 1998, p.2). Evolving from Freudian psychoanalytic theory, major contributors have contributed to this new model of human development, illuminating their ideas through their individual and unique styles of writing and thinking.

As one of its central figures, Winnicott's theories have in part sometimes been described as being 'ambiguous'. However, I would rather view his use of language, and the way in which he chooses to recount his ideas, as being 'playful', allowing one to join him in exploring the world of the infant. And it is to Winnicott that I now turn.

CHAPTER 2

# The Language of Music and the Music of Winnicott

*If I speak, my words hurt; if I don't, I am useless, and I often find myself questioning what I am saying or not saying.*

(Symington 2000, p.30)

## Winnicott and music

As one of the foremost thinkers of his time, and a psychoanalyst who has given the world of child development a unique understanding of the mother–baby relationship, this chapter is committed to reflecting upon the early life, influences and thinking of Donald Winnicott alone. As a psychoanalyst and paediatrician, Winnicott had the gift of communication for, as Kahr (1996) tells us, 'Winnicott tried to talk to mothers and fathers from every walk of life, in order to help them to understand that their babies and toddlers could be interesting people in their own right, not mere bundles of nuisance languishing in their cots' (xxviii). One could suggest that it was Winnicott who helped us to be curious and fascinated about babies. Discovering the significance of music in Winnicott's life and through exposing myself to his writings, I have come to see a striking connection between how Winnicott used the language of words and my own employment of the medium of music as a therapeutic tool. In fact, I am left to wonder what the world of music therapy might have been like had Winnicott become a music therapist! But to continue.

Born in 1896, Winnicott was the youngest child of three. His household consisted of a mother, a father, two sisters, a nanny, aunt and a governess. As the only boy in a household dominated by women, Winnicott's early life provided him with a particular family experience which could be understood as forming the bedrock upon which he developed his understanding of women and, in particular, the specific qualities relating to mothering. As he himself described, the impact his early family system had upon his childhood left him feeling that 'in a sense I was an only child with multiple mothers' (Kahr 1996, cited in Giovacchini 1990, p.10), which tells us that the effect of this unusual family construction upon Winnicott's development brought about particular emotional nuances. Kahr writes, 'This unique constellation of a little boy fully enveloped by mothers and virtually deprived of a father seems to have left an indelible impression on Winnicott's psychological development, resulting in a powerful female identification' (1994, p.6).

The dominance of female presence in Winnicott's household perhaps intensified the absence of a strong male figure. For, as Winnicott himself described, 'My father was there to be killed, but it is probably true that in the early years he left me too much to all my mothers' (C.Winnicott cited in Giovacchini 1990, p.10). The effect of this particular family dynamic remained throughout Winnicott's life and in fact he did not feel that the parental balance was ever redressed. Things, as he described, 'never quite righted themselves'. The early influence of the female psyche upon Winnicott's development not only affected how he came to think about the early mother–baby relationship, but also how he wrote about it. One of the most vivid examples of this imbalance is seen in the index of his book *Playing and Reality* (2008) in which there are 55 entries for 'mother' but only three for 'father'.

Winnicott's dedication to the role of mothers became expressed not only within his theory of human development, but also in the various lectures and talks he gave to other professionals. He was always concerned to honour the ordinariness of a mother's duties whilst at the same time as acknowledging its unique qualities. And in his title, 'The ordinary devoted mother', which was chosen for his radio talks, we are provided with a perfect example of this ability. This series of talks introduced audiences to central ideas on infancy and, true to Winnicott's commitment for making complex psychological ideas accessible, created a style of delivery that engaged even those not necessarily interested in psychological theory. As I have already indicated, Winnicott was unashamedly biased towards mothers but, on occasions, he would feel a need to justify this stance and in one of his talks he began by explaining that:

> There are many who assume that I am sentimental about mothers and that I idealise them, and that I leave out fathers, and that I can't see that some mothers are pretty awful if not impossible. I have to put up with these small inconveniences because I am not ashamed of what is implied by these words. (Winnicott 1988, p.4)

One of the criticisms directed at Winnicott has been to do with the emphasis in his writings upon the exclusivity of the mother–baby pairing. So it is not surprising that this bias does not sit easily within the world of fathers. But if we study his theories, then I would suggest that we also have to hold in mind his family system, which clearly influenced his thinking and which is probably responsible for his ability to bring to life, in a particular and vivid way, his observations and understandings of the mothering role. It is in part our limitations which help to make us who we are and, in Winnicott's case, the absent father could be the restriction which as a man, helped to make his understanding of the sensitivities of mothering so unique. As ever in a playful style and in an attempt to clarify his focus, Winnicott delivers a talk entitled 'A Man Looks at Motherhood', in which he tells his audience, 'I am a man, so I can never really know what it is like to see wrapped up over there in the cot a bit of my own self. Only a woman can experience this' (Winnicott 1971, p.15).

I would suggest that perhaps we could consider Winnicott as the forerunner of the male liberation movement! That through the absence of a strong father presence in his theories, coupled with his emphasis on the role of mother, Winnicott has paradoxically drawn our attention to its place or, should I say, the space a father holds in a family. In other words, we notice the gap. One could say that the male absence in his writings becomes the 'elephant in the room' (an animal for which I have the greatest respect!).

Continuing the reference to a gap or, as Phillips describes, 'spaces between' (1988, p.2) links to one of Winnicott's important preoccupations and one which led him to create one of his most significant concepts: transitional objects and phenomena. Discovering the writings of Darwin in his early years, Winnicott became taken with the concept of the evolutionary gap. He writes that: 'I could not leave off reading it…it showed me that gaps in knowledge and understanding need not scare me. For me this idea meant a great lessening of tension and consequently a release of energy for work and play' (Davis and Wallbridge 1981, p.8).

So here we have the concept of a gap, which for some could be terrifying, but for Winnicott affords him the space in which he can play. And play and playing is central not only to Winnicott's life, but becomes central to his thinking about early development. For Winnicott, an ability to play was central to healthy development. In fact Winnicott believed that if a patient in therapy could not play then 'the therapist must attend to this major symptom before interpreting fragments of behaviour' (Winnicott 2008, p.64). We discover that the origins of this preoccupation with playing had been fostered in his early life. And growing up in the Winnicott household, as his wife tells us, he was able to 'fill the spaces with bits of himself and so gradually to make his world his own' (1990, p.8).

One of the activities with which Winnicott chose to fill these spaces was music and he took great pleasure in listening to this medium, as well as performing. His musical self was expressed through his singing and by playing the piano. More informally, we learn from a close friend that Winnicott 'loved to sing to himself whenever he walked up or down the stairs' (Kahr 1996, p.105). In addition to his skills in voice and piano, Winnicott also learned the recorder, and later on expressed a desire to write a musical comedy. His favourite composers were Bach and Beethoven and, as a demonstration of his versatility and playfulness, we learn that he also liked the Beatles. In fact Clare, his second wife, describes that music was 'a joy to both of us' (Giovancchini 1990, p.17). Significantly and in relation to the theme of this chapter, we learn that it was as if 'the refinement and abstraction of the musical idiom… Helped him to gather in and realize in himself the rich harvest of a lifetime' (p.17).

As a medium central to Winncott's daily life, he would often play the piano between patients, and at the close of a day's work, would 'celebrate the end…by a musical outburst fortissimo' (p.17). It is interesting to imagine Winnicott concluding his day's clinical practice, which would have been carried out predominantly in the language of words, with a kind of musical cadenza. Perhaps by ending with music, Winnicott was using this medium transformationally. By placing a day's verbal conscious and unconscious expressions into the non-verbal language of music he was making notes of a very different kind!

As well as his personal interest in this art form, Winnicott would 'pepper his lectures with references'. And arising from a direct communication from Irmi Elkan in 1994, Kahr retells how she remembered Winnicott once stunned his audience by speaking about the musical *The Boyfriend*. Much to the astonishment of his listeners, Winnicott described the plot as being a 'perfect example of the difference between id relationships and ego-relatedness' (Kahr 1996 p.106).

The centrality of music in Winnicott's later life and prior to him qualifying as a paediatrician was perhaps the catalyst that fired his sociable nature. As a student studying medicine at Cambridge Winnicott's room became 'a popular meeting place because he had hired a piano and played it unceasingly and had a good tenor voice for singing' (Giovancchini 1990, p.13). Not content to share his passion with his fellow students, when the First World War began, Winnicott helped out in one of the military hospitals. A story told about him during his time on the ward paints an endearing picture of a man who knew how to play, even during difficult circumstances. Apparently, Winnicott liked to sing a comic song to the patients 'on Saturday evenings'. The song he sang was 'Apple Dumplings', which, as the patient recorded, 'cheered us all up' (Giovancchini 1990, p.13). Perhaps this was a Winnicottian version of music therapy!

The musical picture created at this time of his life is expanded further when we learn that, during this demanding time of training, Winnicott would often be seen to be 'hurrying off at the last minute to hear operas for the first time, where he usually stood in his slippers at the back of the "gods"' (Giovancchini 1990, p.14). This endearing picture of a lively, active and creative man is one which carries him through until the end of his life. For, as we read in his uncompleted autobiography, 'Let me see. What was happening when I died? My prayer had been answered. I was alive when I died...' (p.6).

As a student, and having discovered Freud, Winnicott entered psychoanalysis. Qualifying as a paediatrician in 1923 he took up two appointments, one post at The Queens Hospital for Children and the second at Paddington Green Children's Hospital where he set up his famous clinic, which gradually became a psychiatric clinic. During his time at Paddington Green Hospital, Winnicott became a consultant in children's medicine, as well as a child psychiatrist and, by the time he came to retiring, had worked with over 60,000 families. His first psychoanalysis was with James Strachey in 1923 and his second with Joan Riviere, beginning in 1933. And, following his qualification as a psychoanalyst, in 1935 he became a member of the British Psychoanalytical Society.

Once Winnicott had entered the world of psychoanalysis, he was able to reflect upon his initial medical training. He realised, as he describes, that this had focused too much upon the physical elements of development and, as a result, had created what he named as a 'block', impeding him from gaining a fuller understanding of childhood illnesses and inhibiting his ability to empathise with children. It was the establishment of his psychoanalytic understanding which eventually came to underpin the development of Winnicott's theories and which was to prompt his move out of the influences he had absorbed from the classical Freudian tradition and Kleinian theory and into the Middle School in which his unique ideas became crystallised.

Arising out of his life's work with children and his later practice with adult patients, Winnicott has made a substantial contribution to psychoanalytic thinking, which, as Abram suggests, 'may be condensed into three main areas: 'the mother–infant relationship, primary creativity, and transitional phenomena' (Abram 1996, p.2). One of the theoretical threads interwoven throughout his writings and one 'not obviously compatible with traditional psychoanalytic theory' (Phillips 1988, p.3) was Winnicott's thinking about the self, which he believed to be at the centre of each person. Phillips suggests that his use of this term is idiosyncratic and sometimes mystifying. Yet these very characteristics are in part what makes Winnicott unique and stimulating to read. In its development, Winnicott refers to a sense of 'feeling real' and in the last ten years of his life 'distinguished between the true and false self' (Abram 1996, p.268).

The unique quality of Winnicott's thinking, his skill in imparting his theories and the very musicality of his communicative style leads me into the latter part of my discussion in which I wish to reflect upon the language of words and the language of music.

We know that words were important to Winnicott and that he was careful in how he used them. We also learn however, that although he was at pains to make his ideas accessible, the ways in which they were drawn together defied logic. Consequently, as Modell tells us, anyone's effort 'to present Winnicott's ideas systematically, comes up against the obstacle that systematic thought was inimical to Winnicott himself' (Modell, cited in Giovancchini 1990, p.121). Perhaps Milner's comparison to a Catherine wheel that sends off sparks in every direction, yet always from a unified centre, is a more apt and for me compelling picture of this psychoanalyst and reflects a form of energy which attracts me to his ideas (Modell, cited in Giovancchini 1990).

## The music of words

I would like to suggest that there is an analogy between the nature of Winnicott's writing, thinking and practice and the nature of music and, in particular, how this medium is used within a therapeutic relationship. Winnicott's ability to be spontaneous and playful in his theoretical writings, as well as in his moment-to-moment verbal communications with audiences and patients alike, produced a man who could be highly attuned to his friends, audiences and patients. In the foreword to Kahr's (1996) book on Winnicott's life, it is noted that having been told of Winnicott's forthcoming visit to his Scandinavian colleague and family, the non-English speaking children were quick to express their delight, describing how 'interesting' and 'interested' Winnicott had been during his last stay. The children, some of whom were under four years old, were heard to enthusiastically recall that when he had stayed previously Winnicott had 'understood so much' which they could not believe for, as they explained, 'there had been no common language spoken' (Kahr 1996, p.xviii). This

Communication

story perfectly illustrates not only the fact that Winnicott was able to make meaningful connections with those who did not speak his native tongue, but that his ability to empathise was so finely tuned that words were not even necessary. Particularly, it would seem, with the younger members of the family.

As someone deeply concerned with the concept of communication, in 1963 Winnicott wrote a paper entitled 'Communicating and Not Communicating Leading to a Study of Certain Opposites'. One immediately notices from his chosen title that, before we even read one word we are in the realm of paradoxes, a pronounced element of Winnicott's writing and speaking style. For Winnicott things were never in black and white. Life consisted of a range of colours that could either be viewed individually or all together one at the same time. Being able to communicate is part of what makes us who we are. Yet Winnicott considered that at the core of this ability there was a fundamental dilemma. He believed that a particular difficulty arises in a place between our desire to communicate and a deep desire to remain private. And he provides us with the example of an 'artist of all kinds' in whom as he describes can be detected 'an inherent dilemma, the urgent need to communicate and the still more urgent need not to be found' (Winnicott 1990, p.185).

As a musician, I find this particular understanding profound, as I believe that its paradox represents an inherent quality of what it means to be a musician. The very nature of playing or performing is one that requires us to expose ourselves to the outside world. However, the actual physical process of producing and or reproducing music, whilst expressing something of our inner selves, can never quite reveal all of who we are. Whilst in the very moment of apparent disclosure we remain at the same time hidden, perhaps behind our musical playing or maybe within it. Winnicott continues by wondering if this particular dilemma accounts for: 'the fact that we cannot conceive of an artist's coming to the end of the task that occupies his whole nature' (p.185).

Winnicott's strong connection to the metaphorical nature of music, I suggest, arises in his belief that there is a 'non-communicating central self'. This self, whilst being apart of ourselves, is 'immune from the reality principle' and yet, 'for ever silent' (p.192). Winnicott is now reaching into an area of our being which by its very nature is unreachable, but as he suggests, is an aspect of what it means to be alive. Bringing in a musical reference to capture this amorphous characteristic, he continues by comparing this element of our selves to 'the music of the spheres' which he views as being 'absolutely personal'.

As a natural communicator, Winnicott used his ability to explain complex psychological ideas to the children and families he saw in his clinic and was observed as having a 'relaxed ability to communicate with parents'. This allowed him to 'offer them good advice and support without undermining what he regarded as their special capacity to understand their own children' (Kahr 1996, p.96).

Phillips explains that language was something with which Winnicott was preoccupied. He writes: 'In virtually every paper Winnicott wrote, he says something explicitly about language', adding that in fact Winnicott 'tends to speak of "words" rather than the panoramic idea of language as a system' (1988, p.138).

Time and again we learn of Winnicott's commitment to finding the 'right words'. In a chapter in his book *Babies and Their Mothers* Winnicott provides us with a vivid example of this particular passion. In describing how the newly born baby begins to arrive at a sense of a self, he refers to one of the ways this developmental feat is achieved. He explains that by bringing together all the 'bits and pieces of activity and sensation' (1992, p.11) a baby is able to come together in its own body. Winnicott gives this process the name 'integration' telling us that if all goes well, what happens next is the 'beginning of everything' (p.11). Aware of his readership, Winnicott is at pains to make clear why he chose to use the word 'beginning': he states that 'we could use a Frenchified word existing…and talk about existentialism, but somehow or other we like to start with the word being and then with the statement I am' (pp.11–12).

His attunement to the sound and meaning a term can bring to an idea was something which did not just confine itself to the words Winnicott chose to use himself. As a member of the psychoanalytic profession, Winnicott's concern over language included psychoanalytic terminology. A specific example of what Winnicott named as 'misuse' of words is described in his reference to the word 'envy'. This term was used by Klein in her theory of human development. As ever the peacemaker, Winnicott begins his critique by initially acknowledging Klein's understanding, explaining that this name is used legitimately in order to explore 'the origins of aggression in human nature' (Winnicott, Shepherd and Davis 1989, p.459). But he is concerned that this creates a particular 'aura', pointing out that the word 'envy' existed long before Klein made it part of her thinking (Winnicott *et al.* 1989, p.459).

In his foreword to Abram's *The Language of Winnicott*, Pedder tells us that Winnicott had an 'extraordinary ability to choose everyday words for concepts', which, as he suggests, gets 'to the very root of our selfhood' (Abram 1996, p.xix). This ability to reach to the very essence of what we are and through words, is a gift and one that Winnicott had in abundance. By using relatively ordinary words to define complex concepts, Winnicott was able to bring the mysterious qualities of the psychoanalytic world into the ordinary arena of life. As a result, some of Winnicott's terms have continued to live on in general thinking on early development. For example, terms such as 'good enough mothering', 'transitional object' and 'stage of concern'.

Understanding how we communicate, I believe, links to Winnicott's devotion to music and the central place it had in his everyday life. The qualities contained within the words Winnicott found to describe his ideas seem to me to be linked to musical dimensions. A good example of this comes in his comments on Klein's term the 'depressive position'. In a paper written in 1954–5, we learn of Winnicott's serious misgivings about this concept, which was used to describe one of Klein's major theoretical contributions. Concerned to protect anyone hearing or reading about this term from its effects, Winnicott warns his audience of the impact which such terminology could have. Expressing his disquiet bluntly, he explains that he considers this term to be a 'bad name for a normal process' (Winnicott 1998, p.264). However, Winnicott confirms its part in emotional development, by telling us that it is in fact an achievement. Winnicott preferred to name this position 'stage of concern', and in the music of Winnicott's term we can hear a more hopeful aura, and one which, as we increasingly discover, supported Winnicott's continual emphasis on health.

I cannot end this particular section of the chapter on the musicality of Winnicott's language without mentioning one of his well-known and poetically playful phrases and one that encapsulates his theoretical ideas. We are told that suddenly and in the middle of a seminar Winnicott jumped up saying, 'There's no such thing as a baby!' Ten years later, he referred to this incident during the presentation of a paper, exclaiming that 'I was alarmed to hear myself utter these words...' (Winnicott 1992, p.99). Yet this particular phrase went on to become iconic in the world of early developmental theory and, along with his added comment that no baby is without someone caring for it, defined Winnicott's particular understanding of the early years. He concludes with the verbal cadence, 'We see a nursing couple'. Once again, by surprising himself, Winnicott reveals his playful and creative nature.

## Music

Music and words are clearly two different languages, but individually they marry the concreteness of their actual elements with the emotional content held within the ways in which their individual sounds are expressed. An example of this occurred in one of James's music therapy sessions and vividly demonstrates the power of these two different mediums and the interchangeable nature of the feelings each language can evoke.

## James

James has been coming to a music therapy group for six months. He is 25 years old and has been suffering with schizophrenia for a number of years.

Each member of the group is being offered an instrument by the co-therapist one by one. On reaching James a metallophone is placed before him. James starts to become agitated. The instrument remains held toward him in an encouraging gesture but only appears to increase James's fear. Eventually he becomes so overwhelmed by his feelings that he is almost physically paralysed. Holding the beaters in the air above his head and turning his face away from the co-therapist, James starts shouting, 'I can't do it, I can't do it. Oh God! Oh God!' In response, I begin to play the piano, gently, slowly and tentatively making sure my notes do not come too quickly or too loudly. Gradually, as James is able to allow himself to hear my music, he begins to literally take in the notes I am playing and responds by lifting up his beaters and beginning to play. As James slowly strikes individual bars on the metallophone, I gradually realise that he is trying to play the same notes as me and exactly at the same time. The piece comes to an agreed and natural end and, placing his beaters down, James is now visibly more relaxed. In words, he then refers to the previous conversation that we had begun prior to our play and just before he had become so agitated. In a relaxed tone of voice, James asks me what it was that I had wanted to know.

For James, it had seemed that the musical instrument itself had become an instrument of torture and, in his mind, internalised in a persecutory and very real way. The music of his initial words that had been shouted revealed a desperation and severe anxiety, which only began to lessen as the music James and I began to play together evolved. The musical relationship which developed, and which appeared to represent a safe means of joining together, seemed to have created a safe space in which James could begin to think and reflect upon the previous verbal communication we had been having at the beginning of the session. Initially it had been the music of James's words that had reflected a state of mind in which he was unable to function and where a world of persecutory images had been evoked. The music of the music on the other hand, had appeared to provide a soothing transition between an internal space filled with fear and terror, to the external world in which we were able to be together in a more ordinary way. When we listen to a piece of music, whether performed or recorded, we are moved by the subtle and almost imperceptible ways in which the notes are played and we respond to how the different sounds are crafted together as a whole. The overall impact of the music therefore arises ultimately from how the performer chooses to express themselves, together with the manner in which the musical expressions are received. Like a mother with her baby who together create the early environmental ambience, so the performer and listener are together creating the musical environment which they inhabit until the music is ended.

Attuning to the variants of the musical elements within a patient's being allows a musical conversation to develop. As with James, through the musical connections created, it is possible to bring a child or adult into a place, or should I say space, in which we can play together, verbally as well as musically. It is interesting to note that researchers into early development often use musical terminology to describe certain aspects of the mother–baby relationship. For example, Daniel Stern, when evidencing the existence of attunement between a mother and her baby, defines an element of this process as being a 'temporal beat match'. This can be observed when, for example, a mother nods her head in time to her baby's hand gesture. In this moment they are conforming to the same beat and connecting both in a temporal and special format. The musical qualities of the communicative and interactive processes, which take place between a mother and her baby, lend themselves to musical terminology, but are also of themselves musical in nature. As Trevarthen describes in his observations of a mother with her baby: 'As in performance of the musical score for a song with a designated tempo, mother and infant share a standard of time (beat) and standards of form and expressive quality for the melody' (source unknown).

I believe that we hear words or sentences within what I would name as a 'sound frame'. The different nuances which shape the way in which we speak, or the subtle changes of expression and emphasis in a piece of music, provide both mediums with meaning. We do not just listen to the notes of music individually, or read words as single elements. We take in the language as a whole or, as I would describe, the music of either language, which brings particular emphasis to its meaning. In my following and final clinical example we see how the interplay between these two languages is literally played out and how they come to represent different aspects of Katy's inner world.

## Katy

In the clinical room two-year-old Katy is playing with her mother. In order to support the moment musically I begin to play the electric piano which is placed on the floor. Suddenly, Katy turns toward me and shouts loudly 'Go away', accentuating her verbal sounds physically by pushing her body forward in my direction as she speaks. Katy's physical stance brings emphasis to her statement and has the immediate effect of ceasing my play. In response, mother appears mortified and tells Katy not to be so rude. During my enforced 'musiclessness', I experience a number of feelings for which I am initially unable to find the words. Something about my music had appeared to Katy to represent an intrusion of some kind, which then became re-presented in the musical qualities of her words and in the countertransference feelings which rendered me silent.

Something of the music and/or my role as music mother impinged upon Katy with such force that it needed to be pushed away. The feelings, which my music and I evoked, were translated into both her words and into her physical being.

Reaching to the core self through words is a distinctive quality of Winnicott's language and I believe provides an important link to how the language of music is used in a therapeutic relationship. And in the preface to the book *Boundary and Space* Davis and Wallbridge describe how Winnicott 'actively sought through his style of writing and talking' a way in which his experiences and understanding could come alive. They explain that Winnicott's sensitive use of language and the ways in which it could reach to the core of a reader 'invited [the reader] to respond not with the intellect alone but with the whole self, including all that is remembered and all that is forgotten' (Davis and Wallbridge 1981, p.xi). I believe that this statement could have been written about a musician with his audience or a music therapist with his patient.

In my next chapter I will be thinking about the musicality of our being and exploring further how music is an essential element of being alive.

# CHAPTER 3

# The Music of Beginning

*It is impossible to really and deeply speak about music. It is only possible to speak about our reaction to it.*

(Reith Lecture given by Daniel Barenboim in 2006)

This quote begins this chapter by encapsulating the deep paradox a musical relationship creates in those who are listening or those who are performing, and are the words of a gifted musician who passionately believes in the power of music. Barenboim's statement highlights the difficulties that arise from trying to put into words an experience communicated by non-verbal means, whilst at the same time having the power to impact upon one's whole being. Barenboim's personal belief in the power of music as a non-verbal medium for transformation became expressed in the forming of a joint project set up between himself and the Palestinian Edward Said. In response to the ongoing conflict between Israel and Palestine, and arising from their joint discussions in 1999, young people from Israel, Palestine and other Arab countries were invited to come together to play and perform music. The orchestra was named the West-Eastern Divan Orchestra and reflected Barenboim's conviction that where 'the open ear has been replaced too often by the unsheathed sword', playing music together can open ears to 'the other's narrative or point of view' and in this case one's apparent enemy (Naumann 2013). Subsequently, this orchestra continues to perform and, in its role as a mediating force, has allowed people with strongly differing views to be together.

Conflict between countries sets brother against brother, neighbour against neighbour and, far from resolving differences, divides nations, and in the name of each cause prompts each one to become involved in acts that would normally be unthinkable.

But war may not only happen between countries. Conflict can also occur within our own being, dividing aspects of our selves and interfering with an ability to live a healthy life. The children and adults who come to therapy and are in pain and distress can often be seen to be wrestling with the difficulties life has laid upon them, whether psychological, physical or cognitive and, in consequence, they can become at war with themselves. Fundamental to our role as therapists is an acceptance of our patients' condition, and to recognise their difficulties as being in part a communication. In a therapeutic relationship powerful feelings are evoked through the various ways in which our patients project their experiences of life into us. Joanne was a young girl whose inner conflict had manifested itself in symptoms that impacted upon her very survival. As a further introduction to my work as a music therapist, I will take a glimpse at something of her therapeutic process.

## Joanne

Joanne was only twelve years of age and had been losing weight for some time. Her parents were distraught as they watched their only daughter disappearing in front of their eyes. Joanne's mother instinctively spent much time preparing what she considered to be inviting meals, in a vain attempt to encourage her daughter to partake of the nourishment her body so desperately needed. However, when a meal was placed in front of her, Joanne would spend much time pushing her food around her plate, unable to bring it to her lips. Should she dare to pick up a morsel, once placed inside her mouth, she would continue to chew slowly, keeping the food stored in her cheeks until such time as it could be expelled.

For Joanne, eating had become an unpleasant and distressing experience and the substance of food a threat to her being. The physical attack Joanne daily imposed upon her own body appeared to express something about Joanne's sense of who she was as well as who she might become. Her distorted sense of her body image appeared to connect to an equally distorted inner sense of her self, which included self-loathing and poor self-esteem. This gave rise to an inner conflict between a desire to live and a drive towards possible death. Although an intelligent girl, words appeared to make little impression on Joanne and no amount of reasoning changed her perception of what she was doing to herself.

Following an appointment at the Child and Family Department of Psychiatry, Joanne was invited to attend music therapy. Initially, the thought of making a sound filled Joanne with terror, as if the very act of putting herself out into the world would expose her to the very fears she was trying to avoid. Elements of the internal conflict that had become manifest in Joanne's bodily war with herself also began to be felt by me, as all I could see was a bright, attractive and promising young girl bent on self-destruction. Joanne appeared unable to engage with what was on offer and, as therapy continued, feelings of frustration and sometimes intense anger increased within me. It appeared that whatever I presented to Joanne musically, whether gentle in quality, or simple in its construction, she rejected, leaving the wide selection of percussion instruments untouched. No matter how or what musical offerings I provided, or the different ways in which they were presented, perhaps as with her mother in the kitchen, Joanne was unable to respond, making me feel that my musical offerings were distasteful. As a result, and again perhaps like her, I too became musically paralysed and unable to find the good enough music mother within me who could engage with her. Reflecting subsequently on my own responses, I was able to see that feeling frozen actually belonged in part to Joanne herself and, arising from this understanding, realised the strength of Joanne's conflict. Deciding that I could not use the instruments to make music, as if they themselves had become instruments of torture, I chose to use my voice, the most personal of all instruments.

Music therapy continued weekly with me singing a variety of songs in different styles. All the while, Joanne sat in the corner of the room, remaining still, inactive and emotionally paralysed. In between my unaccompanied songs, I would pause and make gentle and brief comments about how it felt to be in the room with Joanne in that moment. I also wondered out loud what it might be like for her to be listening to my singing. One particular week and after much time spent with apparently little response, in the middle of a particularly lyrical song, I noticed a change in Joanne's demeanour. Deciding to keep singing, I began to hear a small but distinct melody coming from Joanne as she began to join in. When the song finished there was a brief and intense silence, which was broken when Joanne began to explain to me that this was a song her gran had sung to her when she was small. In that brief musical instant, the internal conflict within Joanne had eased, allowing her to take in and connect with a part of her own being which was emotionally alive. Alongside this experience, the tension in the room momentarily subsided, as a real and alive connection tentatively began to form between Joanne and me. As therapy continued, I was able to encourage Joanne further to talk about what she was feeling and, as this element of our relationship evolved, trust in our therapeutic alliance began to form.

With much patience and short verbal exchanges, I eventually discovered that Joanne had been very close to her grandmother, who had died a year previously in very upsetting and difficult circumstances. Believing that they were protecting their daughter, and as she was coming to the end of her life, Joanne's parents had decided not to let Joanne see her gran. This had deeply affected her, leaving her feeling angry and confused. The family dynamics provoked by this event had clearly contributed to the strength of feelings experienced both by Joanne as well as her mother. For it emerged that Joanne had already had a difficult relationship with her mother prior to this event, and that Joanne's mother had herself experienced a difficult dynamic with Joanne's gran, her mother. The death of this mother/grandmother had appeared to intensify the difficulties between mother and daughter, bringing to a head the need for Joanne to seek help.

Something about the directness and intimacy of my voice as well as the familiarity of the song itself, had been able to reach a place in Joanne's inner world in which a good enough internal object lodged. Reflecting on my work with Joanne, I was led to wonder if in fact what I had provided musically were those qualities observed in a mother caring for and communicating with her baby and that Joanne had felt soothed and held during those instants of musical connection. In translating these moments of musical connection into verbal reflections I had enabled a bridge to form between Joanne's physical and depleted self and her well of trapped and unarticulated feelings. Discovering music that clearly meant so much to Joanne enabled me to find a space in which feelings could emerge, and we could be together. Although only a small step, it became possible to build on this instance of musical connection and use it to create a space in which other moments of connectedness could develop. As time went on, Joanne was able to contribute further verbal reflections on the music created in the sessions and, in consequence, begin to put into words some of her buried feelings. Bringing her frozen self into the music and out into words was an important step in Joanne's development. For now she could begin to reflect upon what she was feeling rather than remain in total battle with herself.

The nature and qualities of the art form music suggest that it can be viewed as a special kind of language. Its mode of articulation makes it possible for a musical experience to penetrate the deepest of human places in such a way, that despite ourselves and in spite of all we may do to hide from ourselves, we cannot fail to be moved. The particular experiences we have created by music we hear or play can lead to a shift in our feelings and changes in our demeanour, which will be observable in bodily responses. Listening to or performing music establishes a link with both the conscious as well as the more unconscious aspects of our beings. And in the therapeutic setting the children and adults with whom we share a musical relationship may find that they are able to connect with those aspects of themselves that have up until that time been protected.

It is not easy to find the appropriate tools in the language of words which can encapsulate the kind of experiences which a musical encounter may evoke and, as we see from my initial quote, this is even true for one as talented and musically literate as Barenboim.

Bollas's description of the ways in which we can relate to ourselves encapsulates and resonates with the kind of experiences which I have in a music therapy relationship. In referring to what he names as being a 'self state' he writes: 'This conversation of self states is often of moods, some of which are untransformed "being states" stored by the individual, perhaps awaiting the day when they can be understood and then either transformed into symbolic derivatives or forgotten' (1991, p.5). I understand that in this quote Bollas is not referring in any way to a musical experience. But, as a music therapist, I consider that through the non-verbal medium of music, which I believe reaches pre-verbal states of being, it is possible to reach a place in the other in which there are no words available. Enabling a patient to express what is being felt by them and in that moment can eventually lead to transformation of that which, until that point, has been unspeakable. Or, as Bollas says, may just have been forgotten.

Music is an art form which has at its centre the capacity to give shape and meaning to experiences and feelings which may be beyond and/or before words. But our exposure to a particular piece of music, whether performed live or recorded, or to the music created in a therapeutic relationship, is inevitably a subjective experience. Whether we find ourselves at one end of the musical spectrum at which we define and analyse the notes, rhythms and harmonic structure of a piece. Whether we do not concern ourselves with technicalities, but allow our whole being to fall into the music and experience how it makes us feel along with the associations it may evoke, we may never find the right words to describe how this art form truly makes us feel. One possibility as to why this is so may be found in the central element of music that we name as tempo or time. Time is a man-made concept and one that tries to make concrete that which is in fact timeless. There are the cycles of nature which let us know the time of year or the time of day. But, more specifically, time can move at different speeds, according to what is happening in our external world and in the ways in which a particular event has affected us. Perhaps because music has also been framed in this man-made concept of time, and is a medium which involves movement, we can never capture its nature in concrete terminology. As the poet Kahil Gibran wrote:

> Yet the timeless in you is aware of life's timelessness,
> And knows that yesterday is but to-day's memory
> and to-morrow is to-day's dream.

(1980, p.73)

Musical expressions are never still, whether we are listening, performing a pre-composed piece or simply improvising. Music can, as it moves through time, connect us to a moment, a memory or a feeling that may have occurred before that present experience. It can transport us to other worlds, lift us out of ourselves, deeply connect us to our being, enliven us or simply soothe. Music has the ability to cross cultural, social and emotional divides, enabling a bridge between different experiences of life to be formed and narratives to be shared. This capacity arises from the inherent qualities of this medium to be able to interact with and connect to all aspects of our human nature. It is possible therefore to describe this art form as being a kind of language. And as this language is constructed in ways that are very different to the structures of the spoken word, the language of music is considered to have universal qualities. Through the entwining of its particular elements, music can cross boundaries that have been constructed by culture, race, gender, age or country of origin. Equally, and particularly in a music therapy relationship, the language of music can negotiate the boundaries created by the defences children or adults may have constructed in order to protect themselves from further hurt or damage.

## Jack

For the past five years, Mary, Jack's wife had been noticing that Jack was having periods of confusion, sometimes forgetting the ordinary everyday things of life. At first, Mary thought this might be due to the fact that Jack had only recently retired and was adjusting to his new life. But as time went on, Jack's forgetfulness became more serious and his inability to recognise what was happening to him a cause for intense frustration. One day, Jack took the car to the supermarket, but did not return for a long time. Mary became anxious and at the point of considering that she should the police, Jack walked in the door looking rather flustered. He explained that, on leaving the shop, he could not remember where he had parked the car and so had found himself wandering around searching the car park. Luckily, someone had stopped to ask if he needed help and together they somehow managed to find it. Whilst relating this event, Jack had appeared unconcerned and almost disconnected from the trauma. However, sometime after this had occurred, Mary was shocked to find the car keys in the fridge and on challenging her husband was greeted with complete disbelief. Without wishing to further upset Jack, Mary decided to go and see her GP on her own. Eventually, Jack was diagnosed with Alzheimer's disease and a programme of support was set in place.

As time went on, Jack's memory deteriorated so severely that on occasions he did not even recognise the wife to whom he had been married for 40 years and it became necessary for him to enter fulltime care. One of the therapeutic interventions Jack was offered was music therapy. Jack's illness meant that he was often quite low and withdrawn and there was little in his life which appeared to provide him with any enjoyment. At first Jack could not remember attending his sessions but, in time and with the help of the therapist, the music they played together started to bring Jack into the present moment, enabling him to begin making more meaningful connections with the therapist and eventually himself. In one session Jack suddenly began to a sing a popular song that had come from in his early life. The therapist moved to the piano and started to accompany his singing. Initially Jack's voice was a bit croaky and rather wobbly, but the passion with which he expressed himself moved the therapist deeply. Following the session the therapist spoke to Mary and mentioned Jack's singing. Mary's eyes welled up as she explained that the song he had sang was one they had heard together on their first date.

Singing then became a major feature of the therapeutic work, enabling Jack to bring his whole being into the sessions. The singing of well-known songs also helped Jack to remember and talk about his life before Alzheimer's had taken hold and helped to provide him with links to memories which had significance. Eventually Jack was able to join the choir based at the centre, encouraging him to feel less isolated and bringing some enjoyment into his day. During his therapy and supported by his membership of the choir, there was an obvious shift in Jack's demeanour. He moved from being constantly withdrawn and depressed to having times when he could be sociable and more present. As he sang the songs he knew, Jack became more alive, responding to the music physically, often moving his whole body in time to the tempo of the song. As his relationship with the therapist continued, Jack began to feel more confident and on occasions was able to talk about the fears and terrors which often haunted him throughout his long days and nights.

Time or tempo creates a particular dynamic and, as the psychiatrist Anthony Storr wrote, 'Music more aptly symbolizes human emotional processes because music, like life, is in constant motion' (1991, p.11). The dynamic framework within which music can happen is one that enables our different modes of physical, mental and emotional expressions to be shaped and formed. The musical components of pitch, rhythm, dynamic, duration and tempo connect to the very core elements of our human nature and, by organising our movements, shaping our sounds and framing our feelings enable us to function as human beings. As Stern explains, 'Behaviors, thoughts, feelings, actions have a musical quality' (2002, p.13). The elements of music are central to the ways in which we move speak, relate, feel and think, suggesting that it could be possible to define ourselves as fundamentally musical beings. The dynamic nature of this medium facilitates a relationship between its specific elements one with another and, arising from this constant motion, allows a bridge to be created between different worlds of thinking, feeling and moving. And, significantly for our work as therapists, enables exchanges to occur between our inner and outer worlds of experience.

From the very beginning of life and when we are in the womb, the landscape in which we move and have our being could be considered as being musical. This idea is reflected in Greek mythology, which views experiences of this art form as being associated with a sensation of saturation and being submerged, as if immersed in water. This historical metaphor directly connects to our current understanding of our experiences in the womb in which as a foetus, we are surrounded by amniotic fluid. This fluid conveys the gurgling and pulsating noises of our mother's body and as Maiello describes, is a state 'of fusion and suspension an indistinct conglomerate of tactile and auditory sensations made of liquidity and movement, rhythmical and non-rhythmical noises and vocal sounds' (1995, p.25). From the moment we are conceived and before we take our place in the world, we are exposed to many different and intense experiences within our mother's womb, some of which could be described in musical terms. Certain of these experiences contribute to forming the building blocks upon which our later emotional and mental development takes place. One of the musical elements experienced by the foetus is rhythm, which in its enclosed world can be felt through the constant beating of the mother's heartbeat, accompanied by the rhythmic rush of blood as her lungs take in the breath of life and expel the unwanted elements of air. Once we enter the world, the rhythm of life continues as we suck, pause, suck, taking in the food we need for our survival. Following our birth, this rhythm of life extends into the ways in which we work out our patterns of relating, initially with our mother and then with those who care for us.

Some of our experiences *in utero* directly link us to the outside world and in consequence to our actual mother. As well as flowing through the biochemical fluctuations of our mother's organism, as Maiello suggests, we also have experiences at a vocal level. As hearing is the first sense to develop at about four months, undeveloped though we are, we can hear our mother's voice. And not only hear it, but be able to distinguish it from other female sounds. Our oral connection to our initial carer not only helps us to begin to build an external physical connection to our mother, but as we can distinguish the different nuances of her sounds, helps us to form an emotional link. Maiello tells us that through hearing our mother's voice, we react to it and as well as being able to recognise it, we are also able to receive 'clues about her emotional states' (2004, p.53). This information, Maiello suggests, leads to the formation of what she describes as the first sound-object, which could be the precursor to our later internalisation of the maternal object. Perhaps, like the early Egyptians who believed that the universe was called into being by the god Thoth, we could imagine that as babies we too are called into being by our mother's voice and that before we even gaze upon her face we hear the music of her sounds.

As human beings we are conceived in a musically orientated environment and our development is formed within a context of different musical elements, and before we have words. Therefore maybe it is no surprise that its use as a therapeutic tool has established itself in the world of therapeutic interventions. Arising from its non-verbal relational qualities, a music therapy relationship can enable a therapist to connect to early primitive feelings and as Pullen (2010) suggests, allow a child or adult to be brought into touch with what he describes as being 'the melody of infancy'. Observing a mother with her young baby, we see many musical qualities reflected in how they communicate with each other: the tempo and rhythm of their to and fro interactions, the melodic shaping of a mother's voice as she coos and babbles along with her baby, or the emotional 'attunement' as she experiences the different feelings that her baby evokes in her. Stern describes that behaviours are not discrete events. Rather, 'they unfold and describe temporal profiles' (2002, p.13). Playing music together with children and adults in a music therapy setting makes it possible to be in contact with feelings and sensations which connect to the moments in our lives when words were yet to be formed and when life experiences were such that words were not available. In a therapeutic relationship, feelings associated with the period of our lives in which the musicality of being is all important, can be powerful and in some cases overwhelming. We have only to observe how the sound of a screaming baby being wheeled around the supermarket aisles by his mother can raise our anxieties and even make us want to leave the building. The baby's sounds can reach into the very heart of our being, evoking such strength of feeling that we are forced to find a way of managing its effects upon us.

Even though one may not be technically trained as a musician, music is part of our lives and is inherent in aspects that directly relate to every part of our functioning as human beings.

Through using music to connect to the core elements of our being, music therapists are able to work with those for whom the everyday language of words may not be possible. And in the following chapters, I will be thinking in more depth about the different ways in which music can become a medium for change within the special kind of relationship named therapy.

# CHAPTER 4

# Holding and the Early Environment

*The term 'holding' is used here to denote not only the*
*actual physical holding of the infant, but also the*
*total environmental provision prior to the concept of*
*living with.*

(Winnicott 1990, p.43)

Perhaps it is this concept of Winnicott's, that is *holding*, which I would suggest above all defines both the connections and differences between Bowlby's understanding of early development and that of Winnicott. The focus of this chapter is primarily centred on Winnicott's thinking on this matter, but begins by referring to the observations that both these 'individuals of stature' (Issroff 2002, p.2) made during the Second World War and which affected how they understood the early bonds between a mother and her baby.

Arising from their experiences in the war and stated in a letter to the *British Medical Journal*, Winnicott, along with Bowlby and Miller, had come to realise that 'the evacuation of small children between the ages of two and five introduces major psychological problems' (Phillips 1988, p.62). But it was this very observation which, as Phillips suggests, 'changed 'psychoanalytic thinking about childhood' (p.43) and 'marked a turning point' in the understanding and practice of both Bowlby and Winnicott.

In his role as psychiatric consultant to the Government Evacuation Scheme in Oxford, which included supervising the hostel workers of evacuees, Winnicott was able to observe first hand the impact a child's early environmental provision could have upon how they would come to settle into their new situation. The child with good-enough care would be able to make use of his placement. Whereas those children whose early experiences had been less reliable were unable to manage and their placement would quickly break down.

Winnicott's observation of children who had become separated from their families led him to identify two significant factors concerning the impact of this process. First, the age at which separation occurred and second, the concept of time, which as he explained, 'is very different according to the age at which it is experienced' (Winnicott 1984, p.33). Naturally, the emotional maturity of a child would be central to their ability to wait, that is to manage the separation and, as part of this process, their capacity to hold in mind their absent mother.

But before I further my discussion, let us turn to baby Ben and his mother. Ben and mother are together at home and we can begin to see how the dynamic between holding and a baby's capacity to tolerate separation might begin to play out.

## Ben

Nine-month-old Ben is sitting on the floor playing with some toys. Mother, who has been playing with her son, decides to get up and go to the kitchen in order to see to the heating of his food. As she rises Ben looks at her and an expression of puzzlement passes over his face. As she leaves her chair mother calmly reassures Ben that she will be back soon. Can he believe her? Ben's face changes from puzzlement to concern and as mother disappears out of view, takes on a more anxious quality. There is a momentary cry as Ben struggles with his feelings of separation. Mother, hearing his sounds, speaks soothing words from the kitchen in a tone that intends to calm his rising primitive fears. As she is concerned, Mother momentarily considers her position, perhaps even unconsciously, but after thought, chooses to continue her preparation of Ben's food. As his sounds increase in volume and the timbre of his cries indicate a state of fear, mother finds that her feelings are becoming intensified. She now realises that she needs to manage her rising anxiety. Eventually mother returns to her son and on seeing his mother Ben immediately ceases his cries. He looks at her, perhaps with some suspicion, as he tries to make some sense of the feelings he has just experienced. Mother adopts a soothing tone as she reassures Ben that he is alright and that she is still present. Ben is able to return to his original feeling state of quiet calm and resumes his play.

In this brief moment we can observe a mother and baby who, between them, are working at finding ways in which they can be together and be apart from each other. This is part of an ongoing developmental process and one which, if sensitively handled, can enable an infant to find his way in the world as an individual. One of the ways he will begin this process of separation is to 'test over and over again' the ability of his parents to remain good, 'in spite of anything he may do to hurt or annoy them' (cited in Phillips 1988, p.67). By this method, his capacity to internalise a reliable, consistent and benign quality of care is facilitated. For only when his testing has been successfully managed can he become convinced that his parents are able to 'stand the strain'.

Feeling held is the psychological process that arises from good enough management of the comings and goings in the beginning of an infant's life. And it would be the war years that consolidated Bowlby and Winnicott's thinking on this aspect of early development, providing the context for Winnicott's formulation of the concept named as holding.

But the individual ways and subsequent theoretical representations formulated by these two psychoanalysts of a child's beginnings would reflect quite different perspectives and therefore distinct understandings of early care.

Bowlby's definition on the one hand had become formulated within a more scientifically informed framework and defined in a language reflecting a more objective approach. Summarising his beliefs, it was the environmental factors relating to an infant's upbringing that he saw as being the '*immediate causes* and explanations of a child's later character' (Issorf 2005, p. 83). Whereas, for other psychoanalysts such as Riviere, the impact of environmental elements in a child's early years were '*remote*' (Issroff 2005, p.83). Characteristically, and using his ability to see a third way, Winnicott, although initially sharing Riviere's thinking, preferred to see the impact of the environment as being 'neither immediate nor remote, but *proximate* causes' (Issroff 2005, p.83).

Disagreeing with the emphasis placed upon oral activities, and emphasising the interplay between the inner and outer nature of development, Winnicott summed up his views in a statement written in his paper entitled 'The Observations of Infants in a Set Situation'. He writes:

> As Melanie Klein has shown, there is a constant interchange and testing between inner and outer reality; the inner reality is always being built up and enriched by instinctual experience in relation to external objects and by contributions from external objects (in so far as such contributions can be perceived); and the outer world is constantly being perceived and the individual's relationship to it being enriched because of the existence in him of a lively inner world. (1992, p.61)

Observing child evacuees, Winnicott had seen that, just as the infant would need to test his parents' ability to remain good enough, so a child placed in an unfamiliar setting and taken from his family would need to do the same, that is, test those designated to look after him. For the anti-social child, Winnicott noted that, even if this initial testing was successful and those in charge of his care were able to continue their management of him, this success would be short lived. Winnicott had come to understand that a child's internalisation of the kind of early environmental provision he had previously received would continue to be enacted out, causing his emotional well being to remain in a vulnerable state. He concluded that it would be the consistent and reliable management of the children in the homes to which they had been evacuated that would be more important than the 'fact that the work is done intelligently' (Winnicott and Britton 1944).

Bowlby's approach, on the other hand, led him to focus more upon the objective quality of care and he saw that this was central to how a child developed a sense of himself in the world, as well as affecting his mental health. He wrote:

> Most of what goes on in the internal world is a more or less accurate reflection of what an individual has experienced recently or long ago in the external world... If a child sees his mother as a very loving person, the chances are that his mother is a loving person. If he sees her as a very rejecting person, the

chances are she is a very rejecting person. (Bowlby, Figlio and
Young 1986, p.43)

There is no mention here of a child's internal world, reflecting
Bowlby's more detached view of early behaviour.

His previous work in a school for children with difficulties led
Bowlby to develop his ideas on what became known as attachment
theory, and rather than talk about a mother's ability to keep her baby
in mind, described this early connection as being a bond, basing it
upon an innately inherited need to survive. His theory of attachment,
written later in his life, was not a 'total personality theory' (Douglas
2007, p.134) and his theoretical position emphasised the external
world of the child and its impact upon what became known as the
early attachment relationship.

A Winnicottian infant was equally inextricably linked to his
mother. But his growth would be seen as being an 'ongoing task of
psychosomatic integration' (Phillips 1988, p.2). Referring to Klein's
understanding of the infant's first environment, Winnicott was careful
to point out that her particular perspective placed emphasis '*apart
from the study of child care*' (Winnicott 1990, p.126) adding that as far
as Klein was concerned she appeared to make 'no specific reference
to a stage at which the infant exists only because of the maternal care'
(Winnicott 1990, p.42).

Interestingly, it was Winnicott's increasing emphasis upon the
impact the whole family environment would make upon a child's
development that would bring about his ultimate separation from
Kleinian thinking and propel his eventual move from membership
of mainstream psychoanalytic understanding to membership of the
independent group of analytic thinkers. Perhaps one could say that
he had finally been able to become his own man! I now turn to
Winnicott's concept of 'holding'.

As already discussed, Winnicott's observations arising from his
early professional practice had already drawn his awareness to the
importance of early environmental provision. Following his wartime
experiences he was able to expand his ideas on the beginning of life.
The concept of holding pre-dates and is different to the concept of
'containment' adopted by Bion and one which Winnicott felt the
psychoanalytic world had yet to recognise. He wrote:

It took a long time for the analytic world…to look, for example, at the importance of the way a baby is held and yet, when you think of it, this is of primary significance…the question of *holding* and handling brings up the whole issue of *reliability*. (Winnicott 1986, p.146)

Not only did Winnicott feel that the qualities represented by his term were not considered by psychoanalysts of that time but, in referring to an 'existing confusion', he saw that there are two relevant influences in the development of an infant. He identified these as being the personal and early environmental provision. The whole process of holding therefore was for Winnicott all about healthy development.

Despite his earlier awareness of the various qualities required by an infant in its early years, it wasn't until the 1950s that Winnicott came to use the actual term 'holding'. And, as Abram reminds us, his good-enough mother–infant paradigm not only created a way of 'understanding what could be provided in the analytic relationship' (Abram 1996, p.184), but also formed the basis of his theory. For as we come to understand, a Winnicottian infant is 'held by the mother, and only understands love that is expressed in physical terms, that is to say, by live, human holding' (Winnicott *et al.* 1984, pp.147–148).

We notice that Winnicott uses a particular word to define this kind of holding, the term 'live', which I feel provides us with the key to its nature. The kind of holding Winnicott talks about suggests a particular quality of care, which is not mechanical. And in making this point, describes beautifully what this might mean. He writes, 'we find that she does not have to make a sort of shopping list of things she must do tomorrow, she feels what is needed at the moment' (Winnicott 1990, p.71).

Through one of his well-known and spontaneously delivered statements in which he tells his audience that there is no such thing as a baby, Winnicott indicates the beginnings of a sea change in the understanding of early development. He defined the togetherness of initial stages of life in terms of being a 'unit' and the 'inherited potential' of a newly born infant, one which was reliant upon there being good-enough environmental conditions. Central to creating these conditions was Winnicott's concept of the *holding environment*.

So, put simply, 'the infant's first *environment*, is the experience of being held' (Phillips 1988, p.30).

For Winnicott, holding was an essential aspect of early mothering and formed the bedrock of reliability. Reliability, he observed, grew out of an infant's repeated experiences of reliable care, and using his mastery of the language of words, he brings into sharp focus the intensity of this process. He explains, 'only on a basis of monotony can a mother profitably add richness' (Winnicott 1992, p.153). By using the term monotony, a word usually associated with a negative experience, Winnicott has brought emphasis and strength of purpose to his statement. It is clear that he is not implying that a mother should be bored. On the contrary, Winnicott is concerned that a mother should take pleasure in her newly found role and tells her to enjoy herself! He continues, 'Enjoy being important. Enjoy letting other people look after the world while you are producing a new one of its members' (Winnicott 1971, p.26). He concludes this eulogy to enjoyment by commenting, 'If you are enjoying it all, it is like the sun coming out, for the baby. The mother's pleasure has to be there or else the whole procedure is dead, useless, and mechanical' (p.27).

Once again Winnicott is able to bring further emphasis to this central element of care, holding, by his paradoxical reference to feeding. And in his statement that '[we] are more concerned with the mother *holding* the baby than with the mother *feeding* the baby' (Winnicott et al. 1984, pp.147–148) we are immediately challenged to question his premise. We are in fact made to think. Although it is quite clear that a baby would die if not fed, Winnicott's emphasis upon holding rather than feeding guides our focus toward recognising the importance of this process, warning us that 'environmental failure... cannot be defended against' (pp.147–148).

As already described, Winnicott's understanding of holding involved both psychological and physiological processes in combination. And because an infant in his early stages of life is in a state of absolute dependence, he is therefore absolutely dependent upon the kind of care he receives.

Winnicott identifies specific ways in which this good-enough environment is created. Initially, it is through the provision of a kind of love which a mother feels immediately before birth and for a short while following. This kind of devotion helps her to identify with her baby, and to get a sense of how he might be feeling. As Winnicott describes, she places herself in his shoes. This mode of being is supported by the mother's initial state of mind, and the intensity of her orientation toward her baby Winnicott considers as being akin to a state of being in love.

Supporting this process of identification is the second component of holding, named by Winnicott as adaptation. Its particular nature is 'active' and could be thought of as a kind of matching or fitting in with the other. A mother's subsequent connection arising from this kind of tuning in is underpinned by a sense of how the other, her baby, is actually being at any one moment, whilst maintaining a constant awareness of the ever-changing nature of the relationship.

The two qualities of care, that is identification with and adaptation, are states of being which are interwoven one with each other and take place in the context of time. But this kind of time is one set in an emotional framework rather than being linked to external concrete measurements. And it is the particular timeliness of these two interventions which makes the quality of care 'live'.

Winnicott's dissemination of early care presents us with the core elements of 'holding', which I would now like to examine in the context of a music therapy relationship. For just as a mother helps her baby to build an attachment of trust through the quality of her provision so, in a therapeutic relationship, therapy can only begin if a working alliance has been established.

In my clinical work it has been possible to see two processes of identification and adaptation as translating comfortably into practice as a music therapist. As a dynamic medium, music is inevitably framed within the element of time. Therefore, that which we create musically and through the therapeutic tool of improvisation brings us into moment-to-moment contact with our patients. We could name this musical process 'fine tuning'. With children or adults who are deeply disturbed, this timing must almost be exquisite, for it can be quickly lost in a patient's need to maintain their defences. Let us turn briefly to the therapy setting.

## Alan

Alan, a 28-year-old man, sat still and silent. His body was obviously tense and he appeared terrified. The atmosphere in the room was charged and, before I could form any thoughts in my mind, the strength of his fears became instantly located within my bodily senses, before I could form any thoughts in my mind. The idea of using words seemed as if they could be persecutory to Alan, and anyway, in my own non-verbal state of being, I could not bring any to mind. Mirroring Alan's frozen state I remained still and began to gently hum. Gradually the tenseness in Alan's body started to lessen and on observing this happen, I gradually introduced a few words to the tune I was humming, describing his fear.

Tuning in musically both specifically and in general is in part created through the musical elements of tempo and duration that are held within the individual musical expressions. This makes it possible for a music therapist to connect dynamically to aspects of both a patient's psychological and physical being. Through what I would name as 'musical holding' and within a musical framework of sounds and words created together, it became possible for Alan's fears to ease and for his body to release some of its tension. Holding him as music mother allowed Alan to experience a momentary process of integration to occur and a subsequent opportunity for some reflection to take place.

Winnicott defined the process of holding more specifically by dividing it initially into three stages and later into four phases. First holding occurs as:

1. Holding

2. Mother and infant living together

3. Father, mother, and infant, all three living together.

(Winnicott 1990, p.43)

In the third stage, an infant is separating his Me from a Not-Me state and at this point beginning to distinguish his parents as being different, and separate beings from himself. This can only happen if he has already experienced early good-enough holding, which will support him in the development of a healthy mental life.

Winnicott's awareness of the combined function of holding as being psychological and physiological, led him to identify their different outcomes. Of the former, that is psychological, Winnicott described that holding relates to being held in mind, usually by mother. The latter, physiological, literally meant a holding onto.

He then subdivides this concept further, by proposing that holding also includes what he named as handling. Handling, Winnicott explains, involves the ways in which a baby is picked up or rocked, but also includes how a mother presents the world to her baby. This specific element Winnicott called object presenting. Providing us with yet another emotive image and describing how handling can actually happen, Winnicott writes: 'She does not take him by the toe. She may make a little noise to give him time, folds him round, and somehow gathers him together. She does not assume he is an acrobat' (Winnicott 1996, p.25).

How can we fail to conjure up a picture the way in which a baby must be handled? Perhaps paradoxically, Winnicott's subtle and playful image enables us to engage in the more psychological aspects of this process.

Following the identified stages of holding, Winnicott moved on to define its central function, which, as he believed, if satisfactorily carried out by his parents, can met the infant's needs. At this point Winnicott is at pains to stress that it is those of the infant and not the needs of the parents which must take priority, emphasising the point that if his parents find this difficult, then the infant will find that he has to compromise his position to the detriment of his own sense of a developing self.

Ever concerned to escape a dogmatic approach to his theories, and prompting us to remember the uniqueness of every human being, Winnicott draws our attention to the distinctive ways in which holding can happen. He tells us that no two babies are held in the same way, which appears to be obvious. But in making this process highly individual he continues to make the point that one baby's holding may be another baby's near death experience. In such a definition, we immediately have a sense of the serious life-giving function together with the potential death-provoking possibilities that holding can bring about.

Unlike the Kleinian approach, and taking into account the significance of the external world upon an infant's development, Winnicott reminds us that life is not just about the internal states of being. An infant is also vulnerable to a world in which good and bad things happen but which are out of the infant's range. Therefore the ways in which a mother manages the infant's early environment as a whole could mean the difference between healthy or unhealthy growth. From the start, a baby is on the journey of becoming a self and is constantly working on moving from a state of total dependence to one of relative independence. The success of this process is ultimately grounded in the ways in which a mother is able to orientate herself toward her baby.

It therefore behoves every parent that sensitive holding and handling must be carried out if his or her baby is to be helped to manage what life will bring.

In the therapeutic relationship and as an indicator of the stage of emotional development at which our patients have arrived, it is important that we notice the kind of environment a child or adult will create for himself within the music therapy setting. The various ways in which 'he discovers and uses what he finds' (Phillips 1998, p.74) will arise out of his experiences of the early environmental provision' and will help us understand at what point it has failed.

## Music therapy

Winnicott's two concepts of *identification* and *adaptation* I believe translate comfortably into the language of the music therapy setting and in consequence as part of the process of developing a music therapy relationship. Music by nature is an art form comprised of non-verbal elements and as a medium experienced in time can connect to our more primitive and therefore pre-verbal selves. Within a musical relationship, adapting to and identifying with our patients can help to form the core elements of the initial stages of a music therapy relationship and, interwoven together, begin to create a state of musical holding, which I shall now illustrate.

Musical holding can be observed as happening in two ways. First, through the external environment created through the music therapy setting with all its components. And second, within an emotional framework. As music mother the ways in which I respond to how a child or adult has chosen to represent elements of their internal processes may create what I have termed a 'musical skin'. This can be achieved by responding to:

- the actual physical and musical expressions created by therapist and child together

- the feeling aspect of the musical expressions

and

- the way in which a child may use the whole music therapy environment, which includes the therapist, the instruments, the music and other non-musical objects in the room.

## Daniela: Identification in music therapy

Daniela, a child of three-and-a-half years old, had been diagnosed with communication and language difficulties. Her nursery reported that she often bumped into objects and would frequently fall over as she tried to make her way across a room or around the different toys and pieces of furniture scattered about. Despite her age, Daniela had little language and made sounds similar to those heard by a baby. On medical examination, Daniela was found not to have any obvious physical cause for her difficulties and was subsequently referred to music therapy.

In her first session Daniela threw herself down onto the floor and picked up a cabassa. My immediate response was to literally bring myself to her level and, bending down, turned my body to face her. I accompanied the adjustment of my position with verbal commentary on how Daniela was playing, using a sing song voice. My sounds were amplified, rising and falling in order to bring emphasis to my words. In response, Daniela vocalised an acknowledgement, but then disrupted our brief connection by suddenly standing up and making for the piano. She threw herself at the instrument and, banging down her hands, played a series of cluster chords. Attempting to keep up, I quickly moved over to the piano and sitting down beside her began to match the quality of her sounds, timing my music to fit in with the tempo and duration of her chords. Reaching for a firmer connection I sang her name. But this only seemed to upset her and as a result Daniela began to cry. I stopped playing and, whilst trying to comfort her, became aware that I was beginning to feel anxious. My response to this feeling, which was clearly part of the countertransference relationship, was to remind Daniela that her mother was waiting for her upstairs. She calmed, and leaving my side, squeezed herself awkwardly between the large drum and cymbal. Daniela reached for the guitar, which was between the two instruments and placed against the end of the piano. Up until that moment, Daniela's musical gestures had been expressed in short bursts of sound, barely allowing me time to connect before they were disrupted. During this period, it was noticeable that Daniela had been continually on the move, which considering that it was the beginning of the session and only a few short minutes had passed, caused me to experience an increasing sense of exhaustion. Reflecting upon the tone of Daniela's initial crying, whilst obviously distressed, the quality of her cries seemed to suggest that she was not altogether upset. For at the same time as expressing her distress, Daniela had been reaching for another instrument, displaying simultaneous discomfort and curiosity for her environment. Daniela's behaviour seemed to indicate an ambivalence with regard to the music therapy setting, which led me to wonder whether she felt divided between being with her biological mother and playing with her new music mother.

Once she had reached the guitar, Daniela's upset had immediately calmed. Somehow, whilst battling with her upset-ness it appeared that Daniela had managed to hold onto her curiosity about her present musical environment. And, up until this moment, the music of our togetherness had not only been expressed in our actual play, but also in the way I had initially found myself speaking verbally to Daniela.

Following her momentary disturbance, and gathering herself together, Daniela lifted up the guitar. This instrument seemed too big for Daniela to hold and for a moment she struggled not to drop it. Feelings of anxiety began to arise as a sense that damage was about to occur emerged. Leaving her corner, Daniela wielded the guitar above her head and, feeling that I needed to support her efforts, I intervened, lifting it away from her. Reluctant to let it go, however, Daniela clung on, wrapping her fingers tightly around the strings. Her action prevented a sound from coming out, prompting me to intervene. But rather than allowing Daniela to discover for herself how to make the strings vibrate, I intervened, choosing to pluck them myself. As I began to explain what I was doing, once again I observed that my verbal commentary had the uncharacteristic quality of a sing song sound. However, my interference appeared to be the final straw for Daniela and in apparent protest she burst into tears. This time she appeared inconsolable and even though Daniela had been used to attending nursery regularly without her mother, I decided that her crying was now expressing a degree of upset that required mother's presence.

## Reflections

My anxiety and concern over the apparent danger in which the instrumental element of the environment had been placed, coupled with my need to tell Daniela what she needed to do, had created a quality of relational music that reflected the characteristics of a highly protective music mother with her child. The mother–baby character of our relationship appeared underscored by the amplified tone of my regular verbal interventions, which I considered was a way of speaking usually adopted by parents of a young baby. But by allowing Daniela to take hold of the music therapy setting and use it as she needed, up to a point, I had allowed us to recreate something of Daniela's internal world, of which I was now a part. In so doing, I was able to experience something of Daniela and her mother's current relationship and, through allowing myself to be led spontaneously by Daniela's way of behaving, I had learned directly and intensely what it was like to be her. As a result, I began to gain a sense that what Daniela might be needing was a holding environment and one in which she could have space to play. Through identifying with aspects of the internal music of Daniela's inner world, I had been able to gain a sense of her object relational early experiences.

## Adaptation

Following the beginning of this initial session, I felt it necessary to invite mother to join us and, in so doing, dramatically changed the dynamic between Daniela and me. Once mother was settled in her seat I began to gently improvise on the piano. It became noticeable that from the moment of mother's entry to the environment all Daniela's musical gestures became directed toward her, whilst I was left sitting at the piano, feeling like a spare music mother, waiting in the wings. However, I was interested to observe that whilst focusing her visual attention and physical body toward her mother, Daniela's musical playing had expanded, becoming intense and more focused. She played with much physical energy, as if the presence of her mother had brought her to life. Or perhaps, in consideration, it was the other way around, and Daniela was trying to bring her mother alive. Playing a glissando on the piano I paused, allowing a space in which Daniela could play. She responded by reaching toward the keyboard and hitting a few individual notes at the base end followed by some beats on the drum, which was standing next to it. Immediately her gesture had been completed, Daniela turned to face her mother appearing to look for a reaction of some kind and responding mother made positive comments about her music. Prompted by this connection, I offered a second musical gesture elaborating on the initial phrase, taking it beyond the original glissando. Daniela turned from her mother and, bringing herself physically nearer to me, played an extended response on the drum, followed by a single hit on the cymbal. This created some phrasing to her music, albeit briefly, and provided me with a glimpse of a less chaotic and more co-ordinated part of Daniela, and one who could physically shape her sounds. Once again, following our brief musical connection, Daniela repeated her previous behaviour and immediately turned to face her mother. These to and fro musical exchanges, accompanied by alternate connections first with me then mother, continued for much of the next part of the session, until we were accidentally interrupted by another child trying to enter the room. This disruption was intensified further by the fact that mother got up to close the door. Daniela's response was to dissolve into tears, indicating the seriousness of mother's action. For Daniela, this relatively mild disturbance, coupled with mother's movement toward the door, had been experienced as being potentially life threatening, eliciting an immediate response of distress.

Once we had all recovered from the interruption to the session, and Daniela was sure that she would not be abandoned, she placed her body more fully at the piano and facing the keyboard began to play the keys with both hands. Throwing her whole body into her musical play, her music expanded from its occasional fragmented notes into longer and more shaped phrases, consisting of dissonant chords and banged out in a baby-like manner with flat hands. At times there was even some turn-taking, with Daniela and me playing alternate sounds. As Daniela's full-bodied musical play continued, she began to worm her way up to the top end of the piano where she eventually rested, sitting down on a chair. This shift in her position meant that I had now been placed between mother and Daniela, both musically and perhaps now relationally. At this point our music became more intense, as we became locked into a shared musical dialogue with its own shape and coherence.

Like a bud beginning to open, suddenly a recognisable tune began to emerge. My music had now become march-like in quality and tempo and, as it developed, Daniela began to move in her chair, bouncing up and down in time. She had made full bodily connections with the music and also with her music mother. Playing together and supported by the same tempo, Daniela had become fully connected to her body and therefore to her self.

Perhaps reflecting Daniela's earlier ambivalence, almost in the same moment as this musical holding took place, the previous internal dilemma showed itself once more, as she turned away from the piano and made toward her mother. It seemed that only her literal tripping over the bongos redirected her away from her mother and back into the musical environment.

### Further reflections

A significant element relating to the process of *adaptation* is the timing of a mother's interventions. The ways in which a mother carries out her mothering role, includes such activities as the how of her feeding process as well as the when. These two elements are based within the concept of time or tempo and as Winnicott reminds us, if this is too quick then her baby may experience a sense of intrusion. If, on the other hand, feeding is too slow, then her baby may feel as if nothing is there. He may feel starved. Too big a gap and an infant can feel 'infinitely dropped'. 'Too long' in Winnicottian terms relates to the particular internal clock of every baby. So that when things go wrong and the mother is mismatched in her care, the baby may develop a state of mind in which the only reality becomes the gap.

Timing appeared to be a significant element of my relationship with Daniela. During our play together, I was acutely aware of the need to time my responses carefully. Equally, the chaotic and sporadic nature of Daniela's initial play had evoked in me the need to provide her initial apparent arbitrary musical gestures with meaning. Some of this was achieved by matching Daniela's actual timing of her sounds, albeit with a different timbre, and by extending the short sound bursts of play into longer musical phrases. Through our developing connections, I was able to provide a musical framework within which Daniela's disorganised sounds could be contained and my 'musical arms' could help to build the beginnings of a shared musical dialogue in which Daniela could also feel emotionally held.

Throughout this brief time together, aspects of Daniela's inner world had been observed through all the various ways in which she had used the musical setting. Some aspects had become expressed directly through the musical exchanges. Others emerged through the ways she handled the actual musical environment. My concern over whether the guitar would be harmed had perhaps in part connected to the external awkwardness of Daniela's actual physical movements that had felt precarious, creating an atmosphere of impending disaster. In fact, not long after mother had joined us, and as if to emphasise this element, Daniela had tripped dramatically over the xylophone, landing upon the floor but without harm either to her or the instrument. In response, biological mother and me as music mother had jumped up to support her, simultaneously emitting comforting sounds as Daniela recovered her physical and also perhaps emotional balance.

Daniela had used the total musical environment to show me something of her fragility and vulnerability and through my countertransference feelings, which as a therapeutic tool are discussed later in the book, had made me the anxious mother she already knew.

Daniela's momentary conflict on the arrival of her mother had emphasised the nature of her internal conflict. It had been very clear that Daniela had literally not known which way to turn or with whom she should be playing. As the session had progressed, and for different reasons, it began to appear that both mother and I were of interest to Daniela and that the musical environment as a whole was beginning to hold some meaning for her.

In this excerpt from her music therapy, Daniela had expressed a state of mind which reflected a level of dependence associated with a child at a much younger stage of development and one in which an internalised representation of a stable mother presence had yet to be fully formed. Significantly, being able to throw herself into the musical relationship with me, had allowed Daniela to be musically held and in consequence, held by her own bodily self.

## Tempo

As previously mentioned, an essential element of Winnicott's understanding of his concept of *holding*, is the element of time, which he sees as connected to an infant's emotional experiences of life, rather than the concrete man-made divisions of the mechanical clock. Emphasising the significance of communication between a mother and her baby, Winnicott suggests that at the beginning there are 'no yardsticks'. Rather, for an infant, time is initially 'not measured by clocks or by sunrise and sunset so much as by the maternal heart and breathing rates' (Winnicott 1988, p.95). An infant's sense of being held therefore is formed through 'not only the actual physical holding…but the total environmental provision prior to the concept

of *living with*' (Winnicott 1990, p.43). Winnicott's term *living with*
refers to a time when the infant is able to begin to perceive objects
as external to his developing self and follows living in a totally
merged state of being with his mother. The process of holding prior
to an infant developing an ability to be *living with* an other, in this
case 'refers to a three-dimensional or space relationship with time
gradually added' (p.44 as above). As an infant is gently enabled to
build up a sense of maternal care, so he begins to develop a sense of
a *continuity of being* and as a result, begin to develop a sense of self.
Part of this process involves an infant becoming rooted in his body,
which is the place in which his experiences of life are felt. Allowing
for life to move at a pace that is manageable for the infant helps to
facilitate the infant's process of integration, bringing together his
psychological and physical being.

The sensitive interweaving of these two parts helps him to
gradually develop an awareness of real external time. The infant is at
one stage, as Winnicott described, a collection of various feelings and,
at other moments, 'he comes together and feels something'. Repeated
over time, and dependent on the kind of care his mother is able to
provide, eventually the infant is able to bring the disparate parts of
him together and, by doing so, comes to be 'one whole being'.

In musical time, or tempo as it is named in musical language,
is an element that creates a framework within which other musical
colours are formed. In a music therapy relationship and based on
clinical improvisation, tempo allows the musical connections to
happen between the therapist and their patient in a moment to
moment timeframe and, most importantly, at the patient's own pace.
Repeated experiences of what Winnicott names as *completion (and
therefore non-completion) of processes* (Winnicott 1990, p.44) can, over
time, despite being based in external reality, become rooted in an
infant's psychological world. As the backbone of holding, sensitive
timing can support the development of a holding relationship. For
Daniela, the capacity to integrate her feelings with her bodily self
occurred as she was able to become part of mutual musical play. As
a result, and in that moment, Daniela's experience of being held by
her body allowed her to come together and literally play with me,
her music mother.

## Summary

In the initial quote of this chapter is Winnicott's summary of the essence of the early environmental set-up. The ways in which a mother chooses to make sense of all that we do, and how she makes us feel about who we are, shapes the ways we come to experience ourselves and ultimately affects what kind of self we become. Winnicott's idea of holding is one of the most significant ways in which we are able to develop a healthy sense of who we are. It also provides a way of understanding one of the fundamental qualities of a music therapy relationship. Through identifying and adapting musically, to the music of our patient's being, we can become interwoven with both their bodily and emotional selves. And as Winnicott tells us 'only if someone has her arms around the infant at this time can the I AM moment be endured, or rather, perhaps risked' (Winnicott *et al.* 1984, p.148).

# CHAPTER 5

# The Observation of Infants in a Set Situation

*It is play that is universal.*

(Winnicott 2008, p.56)

This chapter introduces the reader to the first of Winnicott's theories on play, beginning at the very start of life.

A simple but telling observation, conducted in his outpatient hospital clinic, led Winnicott to formulate his thinking on a very specific developmental process. Putting it in its most basic form, by watching how a child discovers and uses a spatula, which has been placed on his desk, Winnicott was able to conclude that 'deviations from this mean of behaviour indicate deviations from normal emotional development' (Winnicott 1992, p.46). From carefully observing how an infant plays with a spatula, Winnicott realised that valuable information could be revealed about his inner world.

As the backdrop to the setting in which he developed the beginnings of his exposition on his theory on play, Winnicott created a very specific environment and one in which his performers could feel able to act out their part, so to speak. He achieved this by placing his props just so and, following an invitation to join him, arranged the participants, mother and child, in such a way that they were within easy reach of 'a right-angled shining tongue depressor at the edge of the table' (Winnicott 1992, pp.52–53). In keeping with his playful nature and along with his love of 'performing', Winnicott's earlier narrative on this work reveals an atmosphere more akin to a theatre.

We learn that there are other mothers and babies in the adjoining room who, through observing the play of the couple being assessed, behave like an audience. As a result, the outpatient clinic took on an almost vaudeville air. For example, Winnicott tells how after watching a baby in action for a while, one of the mothers described him as being like 'the village blacksmith' (p.46). (A comment arising from her observation of the banging sounds he was making as he used the spatula to repeatedly hit the table followed by a bowl.) Winnicott interprets this behaviour to the reader, explaining that the baby is clearly pleased with himself, adding that he is in fact 'showing off', not only to him, but also to the audience. Winnicott adds, 'then with magnanimous gesture [the baby] turns round and gives it, the spatula, magically to the audience' using it as if it were a spoon. Following the baby's communication with one of the other eight babies in the room, Winnicott concludes by commenting that, 'Everyone is now in hilarious mood; the clinic is going very well' (p.46).

Winnicott named this particular kind of theatre as a *set situation* and was always careful to make sure that this setting remained consistent. Its particular nature was of central importance to the process and the performance, 'one in which the child and therapist's use of the audience is integral to the event' (Phillips 1988, pp.72–73). The atmosphere created in Winnicott's clinic was primarily 'determined by the baby's mood' (Winnicott 1992, p.42) and naturally arose out of how a mother and her baby play together. As the feelings in the room would be peculiar to them, they would evoke certain responses from those exposed to their relationship. By including the responses of 'the audience' that were made during the assessment, as well as those of the mother with her baby and mother and baby with Winnicott, he was able to establish that aspects of a baby's inner world could be determined.

The vividness of Winnicott's observations of a child's play with a spatula provided a blueprint for his understanding of a child's healthy development. For, as he proposed:

> What he does with the spatula (or with anything else) between the taking and the dropping is a film-strip of the little bit of his inner world that is related to me and his mother at that time, and from this can be guessed a good deal about how his inner

world experiences at other times and in relation to other people and things. (Winnicott 1992, p.47)

Phillips suggests that it is in Winnicott's first paper, written in 1936, that we have the most vivid and less formulated picture of the whole process and it is in Winnicott's own words, therefore, that I wish to present the sequence of events which formed the basis of his theory. He writes:

> I want to give an account of what a baby does as he sits on his mother's lap with the corner of the table between them and me. A child of one year behaves in the following way. He sees the spatula and soon puts his hand to it, but he probably withdraws interest once or twice, before actually taking it, all the while looking at my face and at his mother's to gauge out attitudes. Sooner or later he takes it and mouths it. He now enjoys possession of it and at the same time he kicks and shows bodily activity. He is not yet ready to have it taken away from him. Soon he drops the spatula on the floor; first this may seem like a chance happening, but as it is restored to him he eventually repeats the mistake, and at last he throws it down and obviously intends that it shall drop. He looks at it, and often the noise of its contact with the floor becomes a new source of joy for him. He will like to throw it down repeatedly if I give him the chance. He now wants to get down to be with it on the floor... What he does with the spatula (or with anything else) between the taking and the dropping is a film-strip of the little bit of his inner world that is related to me and his mother at that time, and from this can be guessed a good deal about his inner world experiences at other times in relation to other people and things. (Winnicott 1992, pp.45–47)

Winnicott's observations of what took place in this special situation led him to define three stages which in his eyes were 'associated with normality'. These were 'seeing and reaching out for the spatula and then withdrawing interest as the adult's attitude is gauged; taking it and mouthing it; and finally dropping it' (Abram 1996, p.291). Putting it another way, initially a child moves from the 'timid approach to gaining some confidence 'mouthing...and live play' (Winnicott 1992, p.47) to finishing with the spatula. Winnicott's enjoyment of words is reflected in the different terminology he uses to describe the initial moments of the first stage. Beginning in his initial paper written in 1936 with the term 'timid approach' and following his next description named 'period of suspicion', Winnicott finally translated this unique and significant moment in an infant's initial discovery of an object as being a 'period of hesitation'.

In the first stage Winnicott explained that:

> The baby puts his hand to the spatula, but at this moment discovers unexpectedly that the situation must be given thought. He is in a fix. Either with his hand resting on the spatula and his body quite still he looks at me and his mother with big eyes, and watches and waits, or, in certain cases, he withdraws interest completely and buries his face in the front of his mother's blouse... (Winnicott 1992, p.53)

Winnicott advocates that it is important not to provide what he calls 'active reassurance', and suggests that, if we can be patient, then it can become possible to observe 'the gradual and spontaneous return of the child's interest in the spatula' (p.53). Winnicott's description of this unique situation is acutely observed and his ability to paint a detailed picture of how a baby may respond to being offered a new object brings the process to life. One of the details to which he makes reference, and that provides significant insight into a child's inner feelings, is of the split-second moment in which a baby may wait or pause before reaching for the spatula. As he waits, certain physical changes occur. With detailed observation, Winnicott makes the subtle but important distinction between a baby holding his body still and a baby holding it rigid. Being still denotes a more alive quality to the baby's behaviour, whereas being rigid suggests a more frozen, paralysed state. During this moment of time, if he can, a child will allow his feelings to develop, at which point things change. The changes which occur and are expressed in physical movements denote 'a child's acceptance of the reality of desire for the spatula' (p.54). For example, his mouth might become flabby and his saliva flow 'copiously'. Shifts in his bodily demeanour release a baby into feeling able to consider what he might do next. Once again, Winnicott's observations reveal detailed behaviours and, as he explains, arising from physical release, the baby is now able to move more freely. Instead of stillness, there is now self-confidence. Almost as an afterthought, he continues his observation by telling the reader about an experiment he carried out in which during the period of hesitation he would sometimes try to get the spatula into the mouth of the baby. But, try as he might, it was always to no avail and even on occasions, in his own words, produced 'screaming, mental distress, or actual colic' (p.54). Winnicott's understanding of this refusal, or what we might perhaps call resistance, is that in this moment the baby is now feeling that the spatula is in his possession, 'perhaps in his power'. But more than this it is 'certainly available for the purposes of self-expression' (p.54). We could describe that as the object has become as if owned by an infant, then any interference on another's part threatens this feeling. An example of this kind of resistance occurred in my work with David, a three-year-old boy who had been referred for communication difficulties.

## David

David had begun his first music therapy session with me by exploring a few of the instruments. Following our initial moments of orientation David's eyes alighted upon a glockenspiel. Picking up two beaters, David banged them down, pressing them firmly against the metal bars. By not allowing them to vibrate, no sound emerged. In an attempt to be helpful, I gently intervened. And as a way of encouraging David to make an actual sound, I tried to lift his hands up from the bars. David's response made it immediately obvious that he had experienced my actions as intrusive and he began to scream.

My attempts to be helpful had clearly been mistimed as David was, in that moment, beginning to take possession of his musical object, moving from the initial stage identified by Winnicott of pausing for thought, toward the second in which he could begin to use it. My interference had only served to disrupt that process, causing an intense reaction from David. By expressing his frustration and upset, David had been able to let me know how wrong I had been in my timing and, by resisting my help, had denoted his unreadiness to play with me at this moment. In consequence I had become an out-of-tune music mother. Reflection on this aspect of my behaviour led me to wonder how his own mother played with her son and whether, in recreating aspects of his original environment in the musical setting, I had unknowingly taken on certain qualities of David's early mothering experiences.

This need for control connects to a child's sense of omnipotence and is one that Winnicott saw as being a normal part of development. He writes, 'The baby now seems to feel that the spatula is in his possession, perhaps in his power, certainly available for the purposes of self-expression' (p.54).

In the final and third stage of Winnicott's theoretical exposition on a child's play with a spatula, the baby drops the spatula 'as if by mistake'. Once retrieved, however, it is dropped again until such time as the baby wants to play with it on the floor or loses interest. It is at this point of his understanding that Winnicott introduces his concept of play, referring to 'the different qualities...relevant to the individual's inner world' (Abram 1996, p.293). Winnicott explains that:

> In classification of a series of cases one can use a scale: at the normal end of the scale there is play, which is simple and enjoyable dramatization of inner world life; at the abnormal end of the scale there is play which contains a denial of the inner world, the play being in that case always compulsive, excited, anxiety-driven, and more sense-exploiting than happy. (Winnicott 1992, p.47)

As suggested at the beginning of this chapter, Winnicott's particular 'set situation' provided an opportunity in which a child could demonstrate any variation from the norm. And, arising from his observations, he believed that it was in the initial period of hesitation, which could be missing or exaggerated, that the 'most interesting variation' took place. Other behaviours that could reveal a child's difficulties could be showing no interest in the spatula at all or, without a pause, grabbing it immediately and throwing it on to the floor. As these behaviours tended to occur at the beginning of a consultation, Winnicott considered that this made them more able to be observed.

It is this particular moment that is *the period of hesitation*, which I would now like to consider in the context of a music therapy setting.

## The period of hesitation

It seems to me that by reflecting upon the nature of this very specific moment that Winnicott has identified we can learn so much about our patient's inner world. By observing the ways in which each child or adult responds to and uses the whole of the music therapy setting, and in the very first moments of being together, we get a snapshot of their early environmental provision. It is important that this detailed observation happens before we get further into the dynamics of our relationship as, once the session has begun, there are so many different aspects of a child or adult's inner world that will begin to unfold and that will bring further complexities into the music therapy relationship. The setting in which we come together, in Winnicottian terms, includes the different elements of music, which are the musical instruments, the therapist and any non-musical objects also in the room. We now meet Olivia, who is in her very first moments of her first session of music therapy.

## Olivia

Olivia was a three-year-old lively little girl who attended the hospital nursery based in the room directly opposite my clinical setting. She had been attending the nursery on her own for some time but had started to cause concern for the nursery staff. Collecting her for her session, I explained that we were going to play music. Next to the piano were placed a few instruments including a metallophone. Once in the room, and almost before I had time to sit down at the piano, Olivia picked up some beaters and immediately played a few notes. She paused, looking at me in anticipation. Arising from her initial sounds, which had an intentional and provocative quality, I felt invited to join her. We improvised together for a while, Olivia on the metallophone and me on the piano. As the musical improvisation began to unfold, Olivia began to involve her whole body, moving up and down in time with her alternate beats upon the bars. Adding emphasis to each sound, Olivia raised her hands and holding them in the air for a second, brought them down upon each note with force. As the music expanded melodically, Olivia began to introduce some tempo changes. These added excitement and energy to our music, driving it on. The overall quality of our musical conversation was sophisticated in quality with variations in tempo, duration, pitch and rhythm. We played easily with each other and to an outsider it could have appeared that nothing was amiss.

Reflecting upon this session, I realised that the musical energy which had driven our musical relationship, had come from Olivia and, in responding to her different musical gestures, I had been brought into close connection with Olivia's musical being. Our improvisation had created music in which we were almost indistinguishable as separate music beings. We were, you could say, all of a piece. But placing this behaviour in the context of the very first moments of the session, I could see that, following Olivia's entrance to the musical setting, the 'period of hesitation' had apparently been absent. Once in the room, Olivia had appeared unusually confident about this new and unfamiliar setting, throwing herself straight into the music, and allowing no time for thought. This moment of immediate connectedness was emphasised by the fact that, up until the end of our first piece, Olivia had spoken no words, despite the fact that she was competent in this area of development. From our musical beginning, and arising from my later reflections on Olivia's actions within the initial tiny time frame, I considered that Olivia had been unable to pause before engaging with this new environment. This suggested to me that there was a possible difficulty in allowing her feelings to develop and a question arose in my mind. What was it that Olivia did not wish to feel?

As therapy continued, it became clear that Olivia found separating or differentiating herself from another within the musical relationship a highly threatening experience. It appeared that our music-making had to be under her control and therefore in her power. Introducing other and different musical ideas was greeted with rejection. Her difficulty in acknowledging some form of separateness was confirmed by the nursery's description of Olivia's issues. Her key worker described that Olivia was unable to share with other children and, more specifically, could not and in fact would not share her key worker. It would appear that in Olivia's early life separation, and therefore differentiation between her and another, had been a difficult process and one yet to be successfully negotiated. Olivia's musical behaviour had been of a sophisticated quality but clearly at odds with her emotional stage of development. Her choice not to speak in the first few moments had brought emphasis to the closeness of our musical relationship, creating a mother–baby-like quality to our engagement and one in which we had become merged. With her initial rush to play at the beginning of our session, it would seem that Olivia's difficulties lay in the area of her development concerned with becoming independent. By allowing no time to pause for thought and finding any musical difference difficult to manage, in her mind we had to remain as one, preventing any feelings associated with separation from emerging. As our musical relationship developed, so this area of difficulty in Olivia's development presented itself more acutely, and work with her persecutory feelings, which appeared if ever I challenged our oneness, became the focus of the therapeutic work.

The special nature of musical connections had made it possible to experience, in a direct and powerful way, certain qualities of Olivia's attachment issues and, reflecting her initial urge to remain silent, indicated that this had occurred during a time in her development when she was without words. In response to her play and use of the musical setting, my countertransference feelings had allowed me to become literally swept along by the forceful nature of her musical expressions. Through the intensity of the initial musical communications, coupled with Olivia's inability to allow for a moment's consideration, I was enabled to have an immediate experience of aspects of Olivia's inner world.

Winnicott was concerned to emphasise the need for allowing a child or adult the 'full course of experience' and believed that this is one of the processes that can build up a good-enough environment. In a music therapy relationship the music created between us and the children and adults who come to us for therapy, can enable us to experience a range of feelings and in particular those which emanate from a child or adult's more primitive and therefore wordless period of life. In my clinical practice I have come to recognise the importance of allowing a child or adult to use the music therapy setting at their own pace, but more significantly in their own particular way. By not interfering or interrupting a child or adult inappropriately, or forcing the musical play in a particular direction, it becomes possible to create an opportunity for a patient to reveal significant elements of their early environment and the ways in which it has become formed.

Before I end this chapter I would like to give a second clinical example from Max's therapy, in order to describe how quite different feelings arose during his period of hesitation.


## Max

In the initial moments of three-year-old Max's first music therapy session, and following his entrance into the music therapy setting, he chose not to create music. Instead, he picked up a horn and flopping down upon the floor, spent some time examining the silver shiny object. Interestingly, my own initial response was to match this behaviour by also not playing music. Instead, I chose to make verbal comments upon Max's behaviour. Following his initial exploration Max lifted up the horn and, rather than blow it, used it to hit two other instruments, one after the other.

Initially, I noticed that Max had begun his session by playing on his own, placing me as therapist in the position of an observer or watchful music mother. Feeling that it was important that I did not play music immediately suggested to me that my role was as a mother with a much younger child. I needed to wait until Max had set his own pace of discovery and until he was ready for me to join him. My initial instinct became confirmed when, rather than begin to play, I chose to remain with his mode of expression and verbally comment upon what he was doing. Despite the fact that there was no obvious music at this point of the session, I consider that there were musical qualities to our relationship, contained within the timbre, tempo and pitch of our verbal connection. Max's initial play had been more akin to the first stage of play, in which a baby is unaware of the other as a separate being and needs to discover the object in a self-absorbed state of mind. To interpret his play musically at that point, would, I felt, have been to overwhelm Max. Affirming a more baby-like behaviour and having completed his examination of the horn rather than blowing it, Max had chosen to use it as a beater, hitting other musical objects around the room. As Max was three years of age, his choice to use the instrument in this way suggested to me the play of an emotionally much younger child and that he was at the stage of learning how objects came together.

In his observation of infants in a set situation, Winnicott believed that the spatula actually stood for something. As he explained, besides representing a breast or penis, the spatula also stands for people. This

*Phases of set situation*

is expressed through the ways in which a child in his clinic takes in the whole person as he plays with the spatula, which includes their mood. But this process can only happen if a child has a normal development. For, as he writes:

> In the set situation the infant who is under observation gives me important clues to the state of his emotional development. He may see in the spatula a thing that he takes or leaves, and which does not connect with a human being. This means that he has not developed the capacity, or he has lost it, for building up the whole person behind the part object... Or, finally, he may see me and think of the spatula as something to do with the relation between mother and myself. (Winnicott 1992, p.64)

Perhaps in Max's case we can see that myself as music mother had yet to exist, musically that is, and his capacity for taking in the whole of me, which included the musical environment, had yet to emerge.

Winnicott had observed that a child might have different relationships with a spatula. He might play with the spatula and bowl together, for example, suggesting that if he finds himself dealing with two persons at once, his mother and Winnicott, this would denote a degree of emotional maturity. Recognising that this behaviour was of a more sophisticated nature, Winnicott explained that only seeing one person as a whole occurs at an earlier stage of development.

At the conclusion of his later paper and having acknowledged his emphasis upon the significance of the first two stages Winnicott returns to further reflections which he makes on the third and final stage. Linking his observations of how the spatula can be thrown away to Freud's observation of the little boy throwing a cotton reel, Winnicott makes the connection between these physical activities and the coming and going of a child's internalised representation of his mother. He suggests that if his relationship with what he names as being a child's *inside mother* is mastered, then he is able to allow for the external disappearance of the external mother. His representation of an internal mother and his external mother are bound together in his mind and if healthily integrated, the rejected spatula on the floor or the rejected music mother, music or musical instrument, can be reinstated and played with once more. So, as Winnicott states:

Thus one of the deepest meanings of the third phase in the set situation is that in it the child gains reassurance about the fate of his internal mother and about her attitude... Something is missing until the child feels that by his activities in play he has made reparation and revived the people whose loss he fears. (Winnicott 1992, pp.68–69)

As with most of his ideas, Winnicott sees a direct connection between what happens between a mother and her infant and what occurs in the analytic consulting room between an analyst and their patient. He believed that just as it is important to allow to a child 'the right to complete an experience which is of particular value to him' (Winnicott 1992, p.62) so it is necessary for a patient in analysis to be able to set the tempo of their therapeutic work. Equally, the ways in which a child will use the spatula, were, as Winnicott saw, equivalent to how a patient will use the tool of analysis known as interpretation, and word paints this process by describing it as being a 'glittering object' and one which 'excites the patient's greed' (1992, p.67). Continuing the analogy, a patient's 'defensive resistance' to either the analyst's interpretation or toward the analyst themselves, may in fact, as Phillips suggests, be more like Winnicott's identified 'period of hesitation'. Rather than representing aspects of a patient's defence mechanism, in the light of Winnicott's observations, the apparent resistance may in fact be 'a slow realisation [on behalf of the patient – my words] that needs to be allowed for, given time, and not interpreted as evasive' (Phillips 1988, p.74–75).

When Daniela's mother had joined us in our music therapy session and had suddenly got up from her seat in order to close the door (see Chapter Four), Daniela had instantly broken down into tears. In that moment of despair and fear it had seemed that her internal representation of her mother was fragile and any suggestion of her disappearance intolerable. Despite Daniela's attendance at a day nursery without her mother, mother's presence had literally been required when, in her initial first moments with me, Daniela had found herself in an internal conflict within this new and interesting setting called music therapy. Yet, following the interruption, her initial anxiety had become overwhelming and the musical objects no longer of interest. Once mother had returned to her seat, musical play could resume, indicating that there was some kind of capacity for repair. It would seem that Daniela could only explore this new setting if her real and external mother was actually present. The work of therapy was to support Daniela in beginning to internalise a good-enough mother's presence so that she could feel able to explore the external world of objects without conflict.

In the following chapter, I shall be moving onto Winnicott's next stage of play in which he discusses his concepts 'transitional objects' and 'transitional phenomena' and the creation of a space in which play can take place mutually between a mother and her child.

# CHAPTER 6

# Transitional Objects and Transitional Phenomena

*Come at the world creatively, create the world; it is only what you create that has meaning for you.*

(Winnicott 1988, p.101)

I begin this chapter with a question, posed by Phillips and one which refers to the point of an infant's development when he is ready to begin differentiating himself from his mother. He asks, 'how did the infant and child eventually reach a stage of relative independence?' (1988, p.113).

Arising out of what Phillips names as being a 'simple observation' and following 30 years of working with mothers and infants, and nearly 20 as a psychoanalyst, Winnicott came up with his most celebrated concept, and one which as he suggests entailed the use of an infant's first Not-Me object. This he named as a 'transitional object'. Recognizing that when an infant has reached the stage of 'being a unit with a limiting membrane and an outside and an inside' (Winnicott 1992, p.312) and that this denoted the point at which there is a recognisable 'inner reality to that individual, and inner world which can be rich or poor' (p.312) Winnicott proposed that there was a third part of life. This, as he described, was a place which he named as being an 'intermediate area of experiencing, to which inner reality and external life both contribute' (Winnicott 1992, p.230). This special kind of space is one that simultaneously connects and separates the inner and outer life of an infant and is one in which transitional objects and phenomena are brought in order to aid the process of keeping inner and outer reality 'separate yet interrelated' (Winnicott 2008, p.3). It is transitional objects which help the infant to move on his journey from absolute dependence to relative independence and, as Winnicott suggests, are ones designated as being an infant's first Not-Me objects.

But to start at the beginning. Growing up as a Winnicottian baby, is as Phillips suggests, 'not progressive mastery, an overcoming of earlier stages', but a 'process of inclusive combination' (1988, p.114). Rather than development being an either/or process, as suggested by mainstream psychoanalytic understanding, and a process which by its nature provides only mutually exclusive options, in his characteristically creative manner Winnicott's concept of development offers a third way. He conceived of there being a kind of bridge that could aid a child's transition from a subjective to an objective state of being, from being merged to being separated, and from remaining in his all pervading inner world to a world which begins to include external reality.

## Callum

Callum entered the music therapy room for the first time. The percussion instruments were laid out in readiness and placing myself at the piano I waited silently. Seeing the drum, Callum immediately picked up the beaters and, striking a single beat, gave me my 'starting note'. Connecting to his tempo and responding to the particularly forceful way in which Callum played, I began improvising. Growing out of his original individual beat, our music began to develop, including a variety of musical colours. The feeling quality of the music was intense, emphasised by the alternate pauses, during which time I was compelled to wait. Such was the sophisticated quality of our shared music that, to anyone listening, they could imagine that we had been playing together for some time. Rising to a crescendo, Callum paused before striking his final beats, which brought our musical piece to an obvious and natural close.

Reflecting on my feelings during these initial moments with Callum, I became aware that our connectedness had been all consuming. It was as if each of us knew what to play and at each moment, yet without discussion. The quality of our musical connection reflected an undifferentiated musical state, and as Wright (1991, p.71) suggests, created 'an almost total fit'. But at nearly four years of age our almost fused state of being did not reflect an appropriate response, particularly as it was our very first session. There had been no ordinary initial reticence and the immediate and total musical connectedness had been one which contained qualities similar to that of an earlier mother–baby merged state of being.

An infant at the beginning of his life is totally dependent upon his mother, whilst she is pretty well fully adaptive to all his needs. This affords him the opportunity for the *illusion* that what she is offering, for example her breast, is the very object he himself has created. It is as if he is saying, 'My wish is my command!' In other words, as Winnicott suggests, the world 'is under his magical control' (2008, p.15). This is an entirely natural and necessary part of early development and links to a mother's ability to identify with and actively adapt to her baby. If all goes well enough, a mother's contribution to the creation of her infant's illusory state of being, along with her continual gentle frustration, will help her baby to begin to move forward on his developmental pathway. How she cares for him will move him from being in a state of absolute dependence, during which time he is merged with his mother, toward a state of relative independence, in which he can begin to differentiate his particular and specific experiences of his internal world from that which is outside his control and external to himself.

Winnicott's image of a circle helps to explain how this internal and external dynamic is expressed. As the infant gradually moves away from being merged, it is as if he makes a circle in his mind, outside which he can begin to distinguish his mother from himself. From the infant's point of view this helps him to say, 'this is a person and mother is another person, a similar one' (Winnicott 1996, p.24). He is now beginning to know 'the inside world and the outside world' (p.24) and, more than this, 'that there is something at the edge and this is himself'. At the start, the membrane between his inner and outer worlds is thin, so his sense of an 'I' is, as Winnicott describes at this time, only a little bit of an 'I', coming about through 'all sorts of things'. 'Such as a toe seen, a finger moving, a hungry impulse, or

Transitional object explanation

a feeling of warmth from a hot-water bottle' (p.24). Becoming a self involves the infant in using an 'I' to describe himself, but also includes anything which 'impinges' upon him. All the 'bits and pieces' of his life, as Winnicott names them, will 'go to make him human'. So the most important thing a mother can do at this time is to keep her baby in mind as 'a whole person'. Then, as Winnicott tells us, he 'can afford to be in pieces' (1996, p.25).

It is only when he is ready that an infant will begin to discover a world of objects. But he has to be able to do this at his own pace. At the point of moving from his merged state, he makes use of what Winnicott came to name as a transitional object. The central quality, and one that defines it as being a transitional object, is the fact that an infant creates it himself. For example, this object could emerge through the ways in which he uses his fist or his fingers or thumb. Later on, this object may become a teddy, or a bit of cloth. This special object which he has chosen will be brought by an infant into the intermediate space between him and the external world, and him and his mother, and will be used in order to help him manage the psychological transition between theses areas of relating.

Although some of these objects are real in nature, some may not be and can even be such phenomena as 'a word or tune, or a mannerism, which becomes vitally important to the infant for use at any time of going to sleep' (Winnicott 1992, p.232). In these moments between the world of outer reality and that of sleep and dreaming, these kinds of phenomena will be used as a defence against anxiety. However, even though it is essential that an infant chooses his own object, more significantly, it is what the object can do rather than the object itself that is so important. The object or activity chosen by an infant becomes symbolic of an absent object, although, as Winnicott points out, an infant at this time is only at the beginning of using objects symbolically. The symbolic quality is more to do with an infant's journey from one world to another. For although the object is clearly representing aspects of the mothering process, Winnicott believed  that this object is primarily one which 'signifies the infant's ability to *create* what he needs'. The object, he explains, 'represents the infant's transition from a state of being merged with mother to a state of being in relation to the mother as something outside and separate' (Winnicott 1971, p.168).

The term transitional denotes some kind of developmental movement and the object is symbolic of how this transition between the individual psyche and external reality is carried out. A real external bridge is a piece of engineering that connects two different areas. Its function includes the provision of a pathway that crosses a gap, which if it weren't there would require a person to jump. In the emotional world of the psyche the space which is traversed by the infant is one that is psychological and requires the help of a mother. She helps her infant to move across the gap by allowing an area of illusion to evolve between them in the first instance, into which the transitional object will eventually be placed. With particular reference to Winnicott's use of the term 'illusion', we find him interrupting his discussion in order to make a confession. He tells us that this word was actually used in the writings of psychologists and philosophers, but as far as he was concerned could be 'something one can pinch, an idea' (Winnicott 1996, p.31). In fact, we know that Winnicott was not always up front, so to speak, about the origin of his ideas. And, writing about the way in which they arrive, he admits that 'what happens is that I gather this and that, here and there, settle down to clinical experience, form my own theories, and then, last of all, interest myself to see where I stole what' (Winnicott 1992, p.145). He wryly concludes by telling us that 'perhaps this is as good a method as any.'

In the spirit of 'pinching' words, or ideas, I shall return to my previous clinical example. I should like to suggest, that through the specific nature of our initial musical connection, and unconsciously on my part, Callum had been allowed to believe in an illusionary quality of his music-making. This had been created through the different ways in which I had played, responding directly, immediately and actively, to Callum's musical expressions and with a quality of emotional knowing. The fact that our relationship could happen without words brought emphasis to the nature of the connectedness, as if we knew each other's musical thoughts. If, as in a later moment in the session, I made any attempt to introduce other ways of playing, Callum was quick to prevent this from happening. A mutually shared space with me did not appear to be possible at this time and the musically merged state demonstrated his need for omnipotent control. But as Callum was chronologically not an infant but four years of age, then a degree of healthy separateness should have been possible. At the beginning of our therapy, it seemed that the space between us could only remain at an illusionary stage in which Callum's need to feel in control was primary.

Reaching the time when an infant can use a transitional object does not mean that he is able to think symbolically. Rather, and as Winnicott stresses, 'he is *on his way* to using symbols' (Abram 1996, p.317). And in elaborating upon his idea, Winnicott continues:

> It is true that the piece of blanket (or whatever it is) is symbolic of some part-object, such as the breast. Nevertheless the point of it is not its symbolic value as much as its actuality. Its not being the breast (or the mother), is as important as the fact that it stands for the breast (or mother)... The term transitional object, according to my suggestion, gives room for the process of becoming able to accept difference and similarity...the transitional object...is what we see of this journey of progress towards experiencing. (Winnicott 1992, pp.233–234)

As Abram reminds us, Winnicott used several terms for the 'place which connects and separates inner and outer reality' (Abram 1996, p.311), such as 'the third area, the intermediate area, the potential space, a resting place, and the location of cultural experience' (p.311).

For Callum, it would appear that his merged state of being had remained emotionally fixed and that he had yet to discover his pathway toward relative independence.

Before Winnicott came up with his concept of transitional objects and phenomena, there had been no acknowledgement on behalf of the psychoanalytic world of such a space. And according to Abram, there was neither acknowledgement on behalf of Freud of there being any transitional process in moving from the pleasure principle to the reality principle. Nor did Klein seem unable to take into sufficient account the effect of the external world. Winnicott, however, had noticed that for a transitional object to fulfill its duty, so to speak, it would need to have certain characteristics, which are to do with:

1. The nature of the object.

2. The infant's capacity to recognise the object as 'not-me'.

3. The place of the object-outside, inside, at the border.

4. The infant's capacity to create, think up, devise, originate, produce an object.

5. The initiation of an affectionate type of object-relationship.

(Winnicott 2008, p.2)

By choosing his own transitional object Winnicott tells us that an infant enables it to become his first 'not-me possession' and, in consequence, he is able to imbue it with meaning. So that his readers understand this highly significant aspect, Winnicott provides us with a little illustration. Beginning in Figure 6.1a by identifying the area of illusion between an infant and his mother, Winnicott shows in Figure 6.1b how this moves into becoming the area in which a transitional object can now reside.

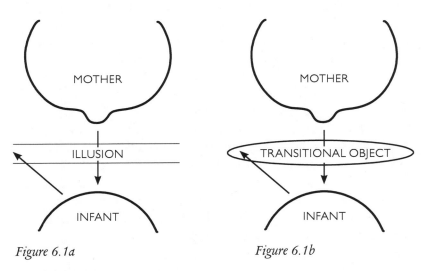

Figure 6.1a                    Figure 6.1b

(adapted from Winnicott 1992, p.240)

He explains that in Figure 6.1a, a shape is given to the area of illusion, to illustrate what he considers being the main function of the transitional object and transitional phenomena. These objects and phenomena start each human being with a neutral area of experience that will not be challenged.

Of the transitional object it can be said that it is a matter of agreement between us and the baby that we will never ask the question 'Did you conceive of this or was it presented to you from without?' The important is that no decision on this point is expected. The question is not to be formulated. (Winnicott 1992, p.240)

Being ready to cross the bridge is a journey, which happens successfully only if allowed to occur at the infant's pace. If it takes place too quickly or in a way that is too difficult for a baby to manage, then it can feel that the world has impinged upon him, causing him to defend against this particular developmental process. At this point, becoming separate can feel like falling into a hole or disappearing, which is a terrifying prospect for any infant. Providing us with yet another example, Winnicott paints a vivid picture of how this may happen. The setting is a hospital, in which a new mother is learning to feed her baby. Referring to how the medical profession can, through 'helping' a mother with her baby, believe they are being useful, Winnicott exclaims that this is something which has caused him to 'tremble when I think how doctors and nurses interfere so easily' (Winnicott 1996, p.30).

I concur with the intensity of Winnicott's response, as in an attempt to encourage a more shared musical conversation with Callum I had introduced different musical ideas. My timing was clearly wrong, as he appeared to fall into a terrified and persecutory state of mind, becoming unable to play. My need to push our music on had traumatically interfered with his sense of our musical space, causing an almost life and death to emerge in the relationship.

By managing to give her baby the illusion that what he is getting is the very thing he has created, 'out of his own feelings, (and) his own power to hallucinate', the infant is provided with the basis for mental health. I would like to consider how this aspect, that is the creation of a musical illusion, arose in my work with Tim, a four-year-old boy with communication difficulties.

## Tim

Tim came for his session and in his usual fashion immediately began touring the room, examining the different instruments that were laid out. As he passed the drum he reached out to hit it and, moving onto the guitar, picked it up and strummed the strings for a few moments. All the while, Tim accompanied his musical explorations with a continuous sing song conversation with himself. My musical response was to connect melodically with Tim's instrumental and vocal expressions, which in the moment appeared to be acceptable to him. Although Tim did not directly or obviously respond to me musically, I did feel as if I was providing some kind of musical background to his activities.

In the corner of the room was a swivel chair and on seeing it, Tim jumped onto the seat and began to spin around. It appeared that as he let his body fall over the seat, the circular spinning movement allowed him to feel carried around. Tim provided a musical accompaniment to his spinning, vocalizing an 'ee' sound, which mirrored the physicality and timbre of his movement as he spun around. As Tim's spinning continued, he began to include some words, punctuating each turn with a colour or a number. At this point, my own musical punctuations, imitations and reflections of his sounds appeared to provide Tim with a platform upon which he could continue his private play. We continued together for a while until suddenly a phrase he spoke caught my attention. I stopped playing and, wondering what Tim had said, asked him to repeat his words. Immediately Tim stopped spinning and fixing his gaze upon me replied with the word 'Nothing!' The musical quality of this spoken word was dramatic, leading me to feel that by asking him this question, I had behaved intrusively. In the moment of my direct and simple question, it appeared that I had broken into the world Tim had been creating for himself and the musical illusory bubble had become suddenly and uncomfortably disrupted. Following this moment of interference, Tim returned to his spinning. Yet despite my apparent interference, on every turn Tim wheeled his chair nearer to me. On arriving at the piano, he reached out and banged the drum next to it. I responded on the piano by matching his sound melodically and rhythmically. Initiating further musical play, Tim laid his hands upon the keyboard. Feeling that I was being invited to join him, I began to play, and for a while we were able to improvise a piano duet. The quality of our musical connectedness now had quite a different feel to the previous spinning words and music, creating an intermediate space in which we could both play together.

'Pinching' Winnicott's idea, I would like to suggest how this process could be musically illustrated and in a Winnicottian way.

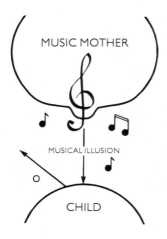
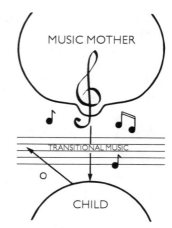

*Figure 6.2a*                              *Figure 6.2b*

*(adapted from Winnicott 1992, p.240)*

It would seem to me that, using the different objects in the room, Tim had briefly been able to move from the space of musical illusion illustrated in Figure 6.2a, in which we were primarily undifferentiated, into a potential space for mutual play in Figure 6.2b. The ordinary question I had asked, in the moment had appeared to disrupt Tim's illusory state of being. But, by allowing him to continue at his own pace, Tim had been able to move out of his musical illusion into a third space in which we could both play together.

Allowing an infant or child to find what they have created can ultimately imbue an object with meaning. Tim's initial created transitional objects, which included the chair, his words and his vocalisations, not only began to introduce the idea of a threesome, but also allowed him to find meaning in the external therapeutic world. In his own time he had been able to move from a state of musical illusion to a place of transitional music. One of the central elements of music that aids this transitional process is tempo. Being able to literally move in time and with emotional resonance to a patient's musical expressions, and even, as in this case, sounds created in part by a non-musical instrument, can make it possible for a shared space to form. The transient nature of music can also help a therapist to underscore a patient's more general sounds, as well as reflect, match and amplify any music that is created between them.

Winnicott tells us that if an infant has not had enough experience of the kind of illusion created by his mother, then he will not be able to develop an objective perspective of the world. In consequence, it will become difficult for him to work out the difference between a Me and a Not-Me and his image of the external world will become distorted.

Following on from Winnicott's description of the four overall qualities of the transitional object he then defines a further seven elements. These are:

- The infant assumes rights over the object...

- The object is 'affectionately cuddled as well as excitedly loved and mutilated'.

- It must never change...

- It must survive instinctual loving and hating...

- It must appear to give warmth, to move to do something to show it has life...

- It comes from external reality...

- It has to lose its meaning at the pace of the infant...

(Winnicott 1992, p.233)

This final characteristic is one that makes a transitional object unique. An infant's eventual abandonment of his object will not mean that it has become lost. Rather, as Winnicott says, it becomes 'relegated to limbo'. He provides us with a lovely homely image of this process when he describes that 'like old soldiers these objects simply fade away' (Winnicott 1971, p.171). We will now meet Peter, a delicate and mysterious child, who tiptoes around the music therapy room talking to himself.

## Peter

Peter could not bear me playing music and often told me to stop. In session 27, he arrived clutching a book entitled *All by Myself*. Bringing his own object into the musical environment seemed to be his way of bridging the gap between the external world in which I was not present and the world of music therapy. The title of his book seemed poignant and was as if he had brought me a message about how he really felt. On the back of the book there were stickers that could be peeled off. Picking one off, Peter stuck it onto my jumper, leaving me to wonder if in some way this had represented his wish to be stuck to me. The fact that there was no music during this time but only Peter's constant private mutterings, appeared to emphasise the loneliness of his world, one in which he was not able to discover a satisfying other with whom he could relate. Like Winnicott's baby, who as he described could only feel as if he was feeding himself, the baby part of Peter seemed merged to himself in such a way that it was hard for him to have an experience of a nourishing other. Peter's difficulties prevented us creating a shared playground in which we could play mutually and, as a result, the musical objects in the room could only be used obsessionally and as a way of holding Peter together.

Moving from object relating to object usage denotes the stage at which the transitional object is no longer needed. Peter was a child who clearly found this process a painful struggle, but perhaps was in some way reaching toward finding his own transitional object that could lead him toward a more objectively based space. Winnicott believed that being able to use transitional phenomena was all about developing a meaning for a life with others. He wrote:

> The transitional phenomena represent the early stages of the use of illusion, without which there is no meaning for the human being in the idea of a relationship with an object that is perceived by others as external to that being. (Winnicott 1992, p.239)

But Winnicott made it clear that this 'task of reality-acceptance is never completed and that no human being is free from the tension of relating inner and outer reality' (p.240). What helps us manage the tension of this ongoing life development is, as Winnicott explains, providing ourselves with our own 'intermediate area of experience which is not challenged'. Which, as he suggests, could come from experiences such as exposure to the arts or religion.

In an attempt to 'get in between' the two extremes of how we might consider our lives, Winnicott suggests that rather than see life as being either about observable behaviours or our inner world, we need to ask ourselves a question. He writes, 'If we look at our lives we shall probably find that we spend most of our time neither in behaviour nor in contemplation, but somewhere else. I ask: Where? (Winnicott 2008, p.141). And continues by wondering 'What, for instance, are we doing when we are listening to a Beethoven symphony or making a pilgrimage to a picture gallery...?' (p.142). It is Winnicott's belief that it is in the 'third area', that is between inner and outer reality, in which there is a potential space for us to be. And in early development it is the transitional object which enables an infant to separate and bring together these two areas of living. For the infant the transitional object is his first symbol and one which is only given meaning through the fact that, as Winnicott explains, it arrives not by an infant asking. Rather it is for him to 'reach out and it shall be there for you to have, to use, to waste' (Winnicott 1986, p.50).

CHAPTER 7

# The Use of an Object and Relating through Identifications

## Aggression

> *Shall I say that, for a child to be brought up so that he can discover the deepest part of his nature, someone has to be defied, and even at times hated, without there being a danger of a complete break in the relationship?*
>
> (Winnicott 1984, p.7)

I was sitting on a train and on my way to visit a friend. In front of me was seated a mother with her two little boys of about six and three years of age. The youngest was holding a toy gun, and on seeing that I was visually engaging in his play, suddenly turned toward me and shot me. My response, given that I had not been killed, was to ask him if I was dead. Hearing my question, mother replied, 'Only if you're an alien!' Luckily for me I was not, so I survived.

Feelings like hate, aggression and perhaps even violence are not ones we naturally associate with babies, and certainly not terms we would consider as having any positive attributes. But in the final few years of his life, 'Winnicott's main preoccupation was with the themes belonging to the role of the destructive drive in object-relating and object-usage' (Abram 1996, p.27). In the world of psychoanalysis these concepts are considered fundamental components of human development. However, once again it is Winnicott who helps us to change the music of the two terms hate and aggression, from their apparent negative qualities into ones which are all to do with creative living. In fact, it was through his specific understanding of these terms and his recognition of their centrality to self-realisation, that 'Winnicott would finally separate himself from Klein' (Phillips 1988, p.104). Developing Freud's idea on the death instinct, Klein had taken for granted innate destructiveness, calling it 'hate', thus placing it in opposition to love. Winnicott could not find 'value in his [Freud's] idea of the Death Instinct' (Winnicott 1990, p.177) nor Klein's contribution which retained 'a use of the theory of the Life and Death Instincts' and perceived 'infantile destructiveness in terms of (a) heredity and (b) envy' (Winnicott 1990, p.178).

In a chapter entitled 'Breast-feeding as Communication' and on reaching the point of his discourse Winnicott tells his reader that 'I now come to what I consider to be the most important observation in the field. This has to do with the fact that there is aggressiveness in the live baby' (1988, p.31).

Winnicott's understanding of aggression involved motility and as an ever-changing attribute was considered by him to be initially located in the body. In the womb and before he is even born, a baby may kick with his feet or thrash 'away with his arms' (Winnicott 1992, p.204). Delightfully and perhaps to soften the blow, so to speak, Winnicott adds, that in the case of kicking, 'it cannot be assumed that he is trying to kick his way out', and in the case of thrashing his arms, that 'it cannot be assumed that he means to hit'. This early form of aggression occurs prior to integration of the personality and, on arriving into the world, includes other behaviours such as biting his mother's nipple, for example. In the life of a Winnicottian baby feelings will not be black and white. So that whilst experiencing an instinct to destroy, an infant will be equally inhibited in his urge to carry it out. This idea is central to Winnicott's concept of the use of an object, and discussed in more detail in the next part of this chapter (Hate). Simply put, for an object to have meaning, it is hated before it can be loved.

The aggressive quality of a baby's behaviour, Winnicott reassures us, is not the kind that is carried out with intention to destroy or hurt. But a mother who is experiencing aggressive behaviours from her infant, will inevitably have fantasies about what his actions might mean. Arising from clinical material, Winnicott provides the reader with a vivid example of how the interweaving of a mother's external experience of apparent aggression from her infant is woven with the internal world in which aggression appears in an infant's fantasies. He begins with mother's words:

> 'When the baby was brought to me she went for my breast in a savage way tore at the nipples with her gums, and in a few moments blood was flowing. I felt torn to pieces and terrified. It took me a long time to recover from the hate roused in me against the little beast, and I think this was a big reason why she never developed real confidence about good food.' Here is a mother's account of facts revealing her fantasy as well as what may have happened. (Winnicott *et al.* 1984, pp.86–87)

In reality and externally, the mother's breast is not literally destroyed. But intense feelings of aggression are naturally aroused in a mother during the care of her infant. These connect to her own violent feelings, which in her fantasies, if all is well, she will have towards her infant. In the spirit of framing his understanding in terms of health, Winnicott makes ordinary or natural the development of aggression. And in a later paper in which he discusses the way a mother hates her baby, he gives permission, so to speak, for her to feel that this is quite a normal feeling. Entitled 'Hate in the Countertransference', Winnicott lists 17 reasons why a mother can hate her baby. And, perhaps by way of acknowledging his own early environmental bias, and as an afterthought, explains that these are feelings a mother will have toward her infant, 'even a boy'.

Winnicott named the earliest form of aggression 'primary aggression' but other terms he used included 'theoretical greed, primary appetite-love, and mouth-love' (Abram 1996, p.10). Hate does not exist in the early stages of an infant's life, as Winnicott considers this to be a relatively sophisticated feeling. But early aggression is linked to primitive love through its connection to appetite. In the music of the term 'greed', Winnicott brings together these two apparently opposing emotions. He writes, 'Perhaps the word greed conveys more easily than any other the idea of original fusion of love and aggression though the love here is confined to mouth-love' (Winnicott 1984, pp.87–88).

A baby's enjoyment of his outward expressions of aggression is expressed through his wish to 'suck, eat, bite' (Winnicott 1992, p.33). And linking these activities to an infant's internal world suggests that, whilst he is feeding, he may also be fantasising about robbing his mother's body and to the extent that it can appear to him as if he is 'destroying the source of supply' (p.34). Winnicott's use of the phrase 'inner world' at this stage of development, as he suggests, refers to specific parts of an infant's body such as his belly and later on, his head and limbs. It is a physically rooted phenomenon. During the early times of being with his mother, as well as feeding the infant will be kicking, screaming, biting and scratching, and this, as Winnicott explains, is 'always linked...with the establishment of a clear distinction between what is the self and what is not self' (Winnicott 1971, p.234). Here we lead into one of Winnicott's paradoxes, but one which, as ever, adds to the sense that this is a complex emotion. He writes, 'If it is true, then, that the infant has a vast capacity for destruction it is also true that he has a vast capacity for protecting what he loves from his own destructiveness' (ed. C. Winnicott *et al.* 1984, pp.87–88).

For Winnicott aggression is a developmental process which changes as a child grows up and a process which 'is the beginning of something that has tremendous importance' (1988, p.31). And, as in all stages of growth, Winnicott believed that environmental provision affects how this process happens. Simply put, if early care is not good enough, then aggression can become destructive, manifesting itself anti-socially. In early psychoanalytic thinking the presence of aggression as a separate drive did not appear and in Freud's thinking it was not until 1920 in *Beyond the Pleasure Principle*, couched in terms relating to the life and death instinct, that Freud made reference to destruction. Expanding upon Freud's idea and arising from her work with children, Klein saw aggression in the newly born infant as being synonymous with envy, hate and sadism, which in his ongoing debate with Klein, Winnicott considered as being emotions that require intention.

Determined to neutralise or make ordinary some of the terminology and ideas described by Klein in his paper 'Primitive Emotional Development', written in 1945 and considered a 'watershed' in his thinking, Winnicott sets out to show as he says that 'ordinary babies are not mad' (Winnicott 1992, p.159). Winnicott preferred to believe that such acts as biting or hitting were unintended and, therefore, at this stage of life, not part of an infant's emotional vocabulary.

His emphasis upon the connection between an infant's external environment and his internal world meant that in his eyes an infant's need for his mother to tolerate his ruthless relationship with her, which is mostly shown in his play, is crucial. He needs his mother because, as Winnicott suggests, only she can be expected to tolerate his ruthless relation to her. For as he explains, 'this really hurts her and wears her out' (p.154). The ruthless self of the infant predates the stage at which he can begin to feel concern for the other. But, in developmental terms, for a Winnicottian infant one stage depends upon another. In other words, in order for an infant to reach the stage where he can begin to feel concern, he first has to be able to express his ruthlessness without fear of destruction.

## Kim

Kim had been coming to music therapy with her mother for a few weeks. She was finding it difficult to separate from her mother, which she demonstrated through her disturbing behaviour. When seated on a chair next to her mother, Kim seemed unable to release herself from her seat in order to play music. Her chair became an island on which she appeared to be abandoned. Any time that mother would try and encourage Kim to play she would scream with such intensity that it sounded as if she were being tortured. Mother appeared almost bemused by this reaction and remained seated passively in her chair. In the hope that in time Kim might feel able to leave her island and begin to explore the musical environment, at this point of therapy, it seemed necessary that as music mother I should remain quietly present. And through gentle and consistent improvisation on the piano I attempted to establish my presence.

As therapy continued, it seemed that Kim was beginning to feel safe and, discovering one session that she was momentarily able to release herself from his emotional imprisonment, she got off her chair and allowed herself to become briefly involved in the musical environment. Kim's aggression feelings became enacted as she started to attack the music therapy environment. She began with the instruments themselves, which initially were thrown about the room and eventually out of the door. Then, standing behind me, she used some beaters to hit me on the head. In both cases there was no actual damage. But whilst all this was going on, it was noticeable that mother remained seated completely still on her chair, apparently frozen and unable to engage with Kim's aggressive outburst. As music mother it felt crucial that whilst maintaining a safe environment, I was able to withstand Kim's attacks and, despite my own feelings of frustration, ensure that I did not retaliate.

In a healthy relationship, a child can play aggressively with his mother and express his ruthless self, because he knows that she will survive. But, without being able to do this, he will have to hide this side of himself, which in consequence, causes his feelings of aggression to be given a life of dissociation. Not being able to express his more destructive nature in a healthy way prevents him from moving on to the stage of development in which he can begin to feel concern. Ultimately, a developing infant and child, who is normally 'in search of reality' (Phillips 1988, p.68), needs to believe that the environment which he inhabits is robust enough to withstand his attacks upon it.

Summarising his thoughts on aggression, Winnicott tells us that through his foetal impulses, the infant discovers his environment, which brings about the beginnings of a me and a not-me experience. Once out in the world, 'the impulsive gesture reaches out and becomes aggressive when opposition is reached' (Winnicott 1992, p.217). Discovering opposition allows an infant to discover reality.

Healthy destruction or aggression is unconscious and in fantasy, whereas pathological aggression or destruction is one which becomes acted out, as we see in Kim's therapy. Her constant attacks upon the therapeutic setting indicated that aggression had yet to become appropriately integrated and, if allowed to continue, would eventually remain split-off. The activity of a healthy infant, as Winnicott tells us, is 'characterised by natural movements and a tendency to knock up against things... The child comes to love and hate simultaneously, and to accept the contradiction' (Winnicott 1971, p.237). Arising from Kim's unhealthy state of fusion with her mother, she was initially unable to make use of the external objects in the music therapy world in a satisfactory and mutually shared way. Our therapeutic task, therefore, was to work towards helping her, along with her mother, to feel that someone could tolerate her aggressive feelings and, through surviving her destructive attacks, enable her to begin the process of integrating her feelings of aggression with her feelings of love.

## Hate

> *Feeling real is more than existing; it is finding a way to*
> *exist as oneself, and to relate to objects as oneself, and to*
> *have a self into which to retreat for relaxation.*
>
> (Winnicott 2008, p.158)

This section introduces the reader to the third of Winnicott's papers relating to his discussion of play. Abram considers that this paper in particular 'brings together the whole of Winnicott's forty years of thinking on the issues related to aggression' (1996, p.28), which was a term linked to all his most recognised concepts:

'the antisocial tendency'

'creativity'

'the good-enough mother'

'transitional phenomena'

'true and false self'

And finally,

'the use of an object'

(Abram 1996, p.5).

A discussion about aggression or destructiveness as part of Winnicott's theory of human development reflects his 'final…revision of the work of Freud and Klein' (Phillips 1988, p.131) and, as described in the previous section, is part of healthy development. If integrated, aggression will lead an infant towards moving from his dependent state of being to a place in which he can begin to perceive and recognise objects in the world as being other than himself, Winnicott's use of such terms as aggression or destructiveness relates to a person's 'actual impulse to destroy' (2008, p.92) that in fantasy and, as he perceived it, provided an emotional energy that created the impetus for becoming a more independent person: 'the object is in *fantasy* always being destroyed' (Winnicott 2008, p.125).

And in one of his descriptions of the actual process we see reflected his playfulness and creativity. In a beautifully crafted poem-like statement, in which he is describing what we might see as being a darker emotion, Winnicott changes its colour and brings it into being part of a normal baby's journey to discovering other-than-me objects. He writes:

> I find you;
> You survive what I do to you as I come to
> recognise you as not-me;
> I use you;
> I forget you;
> But you remember me;
> I keep forgetting you;
> I lose you;
> I am sad.

(Winnicott 1988, p.103)

A baby's 'management' of himself is dependent upon his organisation of the ways in which the external world impinges upon him, which, in itself, depends upon his capacity for dealing with his own internal world. As we have learned in previous chapters, this process begins with the baby being initially merged with his mother followed by his subsequent move to finding ways of beginning to deal with the perceived and growing gap between self and other. But if he is to continue on a path to healthy development the infant must begin to accept that he can no longer rely on an 'unmitigated belief' (Giovancchini 1990, p.121) in his omnipotence, which so far has allowed him to feel in control of his environment. Now he has to understand that there is an external world quite separate from who he is and, if all goes well, he will then begin the process of separation. It is the baby's aggression, which later came to be named by Winnicott as destruction, that facilitates this process.

But healthy growth cannot progress if an infant has not first been seen for who he is. And, as we learn from the beginning of yet another of Winnicott's poem-like descriptions, this special kind of looking lays down the foundation for this process:

> When I look I am seen, so I exist.
> I can now afford to look and see...
> (Winnicott 2008, p.154)

Feeling acknowledged in the right way provides an infant with the basis upon which his capacity to proceed from perceiving his mother as a subjective object to seeing his mother as someone who can be objectively perceived is formed. In other words, at this stage of his life, an infant needs to be changing his perspective of life 'from seeing himself through the eyes of the other, to seeing the other' (Phillips 1988, p.130). The most significant part of this process is that it must be initiated by the infant and not pushed onto him by his carer. If this should happen, then this can seriously affect an infant's chances of becoming his own self and his development will become compromised.

With the hard effort his mother has made to identify and adapt to her infant in the early stage of his development, her infant should now be ready to begin taking hold of his life for himself and work towards seeing the external reality of objects. Winnicott described this as being 'the most difficult thing perhaps, in human development' (Winnicott 2008, p.120) but, paradoxically, it is one which involves the more destructive or aggressive elements of his being.

Once again, and using his imaginative skills, Winnicott tells his readers a short story in order to help us understand this particular developmental process:

> The subject says to the object: 'I destroyed you', and the object is there to receive the communication. From now on the subject says: 'Hullo object!' 'I destroyed you'. 'I love you. You have value for me because of your survival of my destruction of you. While I am loving you I am all the time destroying you in (unconscious) *fantasy*. (Winnicott 2008, pp.120–121)

The capacity to use objects will have followed an infant's ability to relate to them and, as Winnicott makes clear, is not something that occurs automatically. As ever, and in the spirit of the relational model, for Winnicott it has to happen through a facilitating object. And it is in this paper, 'The Use of an Object' (1968) and which gives the title to this chapter, that Winnicott tells us how this process happens.

In a particular sequence and for the object to become something outside of the infant's omnipotent control, the object first has to be able to receive the infant's destructive communication. Second, the object must not retaliate. Only then can the infant come to realise that because the object has survived his omnipotent attacks it has become fully real. Survival allows an object to have value, which implies that once again and paradoxically 'it is destructiveness...that creates reality, not reality that creates destructiveness' (Phillips 1988, p.132).

In order that this process becomes possible, a Winnicottian mother must be robust. And as part of his continual links between the early mother–infant relationship and the analytic relationship, Winnicott suggests that the analyst too must be seen to be robust for the sake of his patient's development.

## Jake

Jake's fifteenth session began with his usual energetic period of sporadic and disconnected musical play. Picking up one instrument after another, he would play it aggressively, hitting or banging it with great force. Once he had made a sound, he would fling the instrument to the ground. As I followed Jake musically on the piano, he took up a beater in one hand and a cabassa in the other and carried out a brief moment of what sounded like a bang-shake musical game. Jake would hit the two drums or cymbal a few times following it with a furious shaking of the cabassa. Jake ended this game suddenly by slapping his hands onto the bars of the metallophone. I became prompted to try and encourage him to use a beater and, as I moved in order to pick one up from the shelf, Jake took off around the room. It would seem that in that split second when I had interrupted my own play Jake had experienced a momentary absence of my presence. This had caused him to run over to the door and hiding behind the curtain, shout 'boo'. Peek-a-boo is a game often played by infants as they begin to integrate an idea of an internal mother with the one they can actually see and it seemed that my presence as music mother, for a moment, had apparently been in question.

Taking up Jake's game, and as a way of acknowledging his need to be found, I translated the physical and emotional elements of his behaviour into music, matching the dynamic of his vocal shouting and the tempo of his physical movements. This led us into a second game, in which Jake continued to hide whilst I would seek him musically. At this point I found myself drawn away from the piano and on to the metallophone, where on taking up the beaters, I began to pick out a melody. Suddenly and without warning Jake rushed from behind the curtain over to the recording machine and started to press some buttons. Our game had been interrupted or, put another way, I had been switched off! I restarted the machine and returning to my position at the piano, Jake hit the drum very loudly. His beats were so hard and loud that any musical response I tried to make on the piano became drowned out. Jake eventually dropped his beater, but then attempted to pull off the hand-grip. When he hit the metallophone the wooden end came loose, flying across the room. As I went to fetch another beater from the shelves, Jake's destructive feelings emerged once more as he threw the broken piece of wood at me. As if getting an idea, Jake continued by picking up other instruments from the shelf, hurling them one by one onto the floor. The session had become a battle scene in which I as music mother, the instruments and the music were working hard to survive. The atmosphere then suddenly shifted when Jake shouted 'boo'. In that instant, the session changed from being one of conflict into a shared musical game. The different quality of Jake's play brought him physically to the piano where, having hit one note, he chose to remain. We then began to improvise music together, sharing our musical ideas and complementing our different musical expressions. The music we improvised together allowed us to meet in a musical playing space. The instruments had now moved from being objects of destruction to victims of aggression to objects that could now be used creatively.

A resilient environment is one that can withstand an infant's destructiveness and in so doing becomes one that enables a shared reality to come about. In the case of patients in analysis or children and adults in music therapy, the therapist must survive the attacks made upon him and, for those whose early experiences did not provide this crucial experience, then the analytic setting must provide an opportunity for this to happen. Survival of the object is at the core of the ability of the infant to find value and meaning in the objects around him and, as part of this process, there has to be the realisation on behalf of the baby that both his mother and himself have survived his aggressive attacks.

In consideration of the actual word 'survival', I am aware that it has quite different meanings according to the context in which it is being used. For example, to survive in the way we might understand the intrepid mountain climber would need to do, whilst hanging by a rope, is in a therapeutic setting not enough. Survival, Winnicott tells us, is synonymous with the twelfth aspect in Freud's description of a therapeutic setting, which he identifies as being 'the analyst survives'. But this term is not as the dictionary defines, which simply means outliving or living beyond. Winnicott's understanding of this term is all to do with not retaliating, and, as he explains, requires that the 'analyst, the analytic technique, and the analytic setting all survive the patient's destructive attacks' (Winnicott 2008, p.122).

Survival in a therapeutic context is, as Winnicott suggests, a process which may actually lead us to feel that at times in our role as therapist we are being exploited. Our patients may carry this out in many different ways. For example, by being indifferent to what we offer, being silent, playing relentlessly, attending therapy sporadically or, like Jake, causing mayhem. Once again Winnicott is careful in his use of language and in the music of his term 'exploited' explains that this is quite different to 'being used'. When this occurs we are told that we should take it as a compliment. As if to make sure that we are still following his discussion, Winnicott suddenly adds a footnote. Perhaps to emphasise the fact that to every process there is a limit, Winnicott warns us that 'when the analyst knows that the patient carries a revolver, then, it seems to me, this work cannot be done' (Winnicott 2008, p.123). Enough said!

All this might sound like hard work, which of course it is. But returning to his discussion and choosing his words carefully once again, Winnicott continues by explaining that this compliment is no ordinary flattery. This kind of 'compliment' he makes clear is the 'ultimate' form of tribute and is in fact what might be called 'an expression of regard' (Chambers Dictionary 1979).

But not every mother can manage this process and in consequence, as Winnicott sensitively explains, 'some can and some cannot carry the baby over from relating to usage' (Winnicott et al. 1989, p.221). Winnicott now arrives at the core idea of his paper which, in his inimitable fashion, is described as being a simple idea. He writes: 'To use an object the subject must have developed a *capacity* to use objects' (Winnicott 2008, p.119). And as in all his developmental stages, Winnicott is at pains to point out that progress is not a given.

Should a child's early experiences be unable to help him integrate his contrasting feelings of love and hate then, as in Winnicott's following example, actual damage may be done. In 'Notes Made on a Train, Part 2', written in 1965, he relates the story of a person, who on entering an art gallery, goes over to a painting and slashes it. Needless to say, the artwork is destroyed. Winnicott explains that this is not an act that comes out of love for the picture. Rather, his actions have arisen because there is a real need to destroy, and he named this vandalism.

In our practice as therapists it is not, as Winnicott points out, always possible for us to be useful to our patients and, should this be the case, then the task of therapy becomes focused upon enabling our patient to develop this capacity.

## Becky

Becky was a six-year-old little girl who initially appeared unable to use the music therapy objects in ways which were useful for developing our relationship. On our fifth meeting, and following her entrance to the music therapy room, Becky suddenly spoke the word 'mother'. This was followed by a short moment of play on the metallophone in a way that created a meaningless quality to its expression and did not allow me to engage with her. Having then wandered aimlessly around the room, she picked up the telephone that was on the wall. The words she spoke did not make sense and very quickly she replaced the receiver. Discovering a flower, Becky tried putting it into her mouth and giving up, moved a chair a few feet from its position. She sat on it and, on getting up, threw its cushion onto the floor. The springs were now exposed and climbing onto them Becky began jumping up and down. From there, she moved over to the door, and taking hold of the curtain spoke the word 'dolly'. Turning back into the room, she picked up the chair cushion and replaced it back on its springs. Finding some paper, Becky then wiped her mouth and turning around, accompanied her movement with the sound 'whee'. Wheeling the chair toward me, she asked if I would push her. I found myself not wishing to comply and in response, Becky pulled it up to the piano and started playing one note followed by another. Up until this moment, the atmosphere in the room was one of hopelessness, and my role as music mother one of uselessness. However, when I attempted to become an 'alive' music mother by improvising with her one note melody, Becky's response was to get up and return to the desk situated in the opposite corner of the room. The quality of the environment was one of meaninglessness in which the music therapy objects, which included me, appeared to have no value. Equally, my non-compliance in deciding not to push her around the room appeared to evoke a compliance on her part to play the piano. There was a hopelessness to our being together and, arising out of Becky's disconnected state of being, it was difficult for me to find a space in which I could be there for her.

One of the primary differences Winnicott observed between a baby who can relate to and use an object with one who cannot, is that for the baby whose early experiences have enabled him to begin to integrate his feelings of hate and love, the object becomes meaningful. Psychological mechanisms, named *projection* and *identification*, enable an infant to feel that part of them has become part of the object and in so doing the relationship between the object and himself is changed. Arising out of this developmental process, an infant can feel that something of himself can be found in the object, prompting an element of identification to take place, which in turn gives value to the connection.

Once again, and always linking his understanding of the early relationship with psychoanalysis, Winnicott sees the parallels between an infant's ability to use objects with a patient's capacity to use his analyst.

Winnicott tells us that positive changes in therapy are not reliant upon clever interpretation. Changes, he tells us, 'depend on the analyst's survival of the attacks' (Winnicott 2008, p.123). Acknowledging that these may be hard to bear, he continues by emphasising that it is our survival and the survival of the therapeutic environment that is essential to the progress of therapy.

Winnicott ends this unique and significant paper by reiterating the sequence of events that form the basis of this developmental process and which I believe should be quoted in full. He explains:

> (1) Subject *relates* to object. (2) Object is in the process of being found instead of placed by the subject in the world. (3) Subject *destroys* object. (4) Object survives destruction. (5) Subject can *use* object. (Winnicott 2008, p.126)

Winnicott's baby finds that in the world of objects, that which can be hated is that which becomes real. As Phillips explains, 'he can only find the world around him substantial through his ultimately unsuccessful attempts to destroy it' (1988, p.17). Successful integration of the two feelings of love and aggression make it possible for there to be 'a world of shared reality' (p.127) and for an infant to reach toward the developmental stage that Winnicott named as being the Stage of Concern.

CHAPTER 8

# Playing

*Playing is an experience...a basic form of living.*

(Winnicott 2008, p.67)

## The playing Winnicott

This quote describes not only the essence of real play but is a quality at the heart, literally, of Winnicott's character. And, as one of the core concepts of his theory of human development and the final stage in its development, it makes sense to present his understanding of this concept by beginning with a brief introduction to the playing Winnicott.

Playing is a term synonymous with the nature of Winnicott and, as we learn from his writings, a quality fundamental to his way of being. In his private life and as a husband, we learn from Clare, his second wife, the importance of play to Winnicott and the ways in which it became represented in his life. She tells us, 'I shall limit what I say to an attempt to illustrate the theme of playing, because that was central to his life and work' (Giovacchini 1990, p.7). She continues, 'but it seems important to note that in his terms the capacity to play is equated with a *quality of living*' (1990, p.4).

This quality of living was one which, as we learn from other writings, not only provided the energy which drove his professional life but, as a core element of his being, formed the bedrock of Winnicott's marriage to Clare. Its centrality to their everyday lives is vividly depicted in Clare's chapter describing her observations on D.W.W., as she called him, entitled 'Reflections'. She writes:

We played with *things* – our possessions – rearranging, acquiring, and discarding according to our mood. We played with ideas, tossing them about at random with the freedom of knowing that we need not agree and that we were strong enough not to be hurt by each other. (1990, p.16)

In this lovingly painted picture of the ways in which Winnicott and Clare could be together, and in further accounts of their life, we learn that in fact the strength of their relationship lay in a recognition and acceptance of 'each other's separateness'. This ability to acknowledge the other's individual nature allowed Clare and Winnicott to maintain a freedom of thought and action, including keeping possession of their own dreams. Their capacity for enjoyment, combined with their ability for spontaneous play, was supported by this acceptance of each other. Or, as Clare puts it, 'we were operating in the play area where everything is permissible' (1990, p.16). From all that we read about Winnicott the man and Winnicott the professional, it is clear that being able to play was at the core of his existence. His daily activities, whether involving clinical work or relaxation, were fuelled by a belief in the importance of a capacity to play. And, referring to an earlier chapter, musical play was one of the playing activities that filled his daily routine.

As a child, Winnicott was always 'running, cycling, playing rugby, and singing in the choir' and as an adult, he was seen to be 'jumping over rows of chairs to join children' in the consulting room (Giovacchini 1990, p.51). A further indication of the generalised role of play in Winnicott's life and extending from the more physical aspects of his playfulness was his ability to be creative. One of the ways in which this aspect of his personality became expressed was through drawing and came in the form of the doodles he regularly created. Initially these drawings were part of his home life. In fact, a doodle was usually left for Clare every day at breakfast. But, should they be separated from each other, one was sent in the post by Winnicott on a daily basis. Winnicott took this love of playful drawing into the consulting room, where he used the 'doodles' completed by a child together with himself as a way of furthering his understanding of their inner world of thoughts and feelings. So significant were these revelations that the creative process obtained its own identity as a therapeutic clinical tool, becoming known as 'The Squiggle Game'. Being playful or, as Winnicott was careful to name this quality, 'playing', was as he believed the only way in which 'the individual discovers the self' (2008, p.73), and his own journey of self-discovery was one in which he was engaged until the end of his life. Confirming his belief in its importance, Winnicott reflects upon its centrality to his understanding of human development, when he writes:

> As I look back over the papers that mark the development of my own thought and understanding I can see that my present interest in play in the relationship of trust that may develop between the baby and the mother was always a feature of my consultative technique. (2008, p.64)

Clare believed that it was Winnicott's ability to be playful that enabled him to come to terms with the reality of his own end and ultimate final separation from life. She considered that it was the energy arising from Winnicott's general playfulness that propelled him to consider the reality of his eventual final moments. Interestingly, and in his autobiography that he had only just begun during the last years of his life, Winnicott himself wrote of his eventual death and in a way that gives great emphasis to the aliveness he obtained from being playful. He wrote: 'Let me see. What was happening when I died? My prayer had been answered. I was alive when I died' (Winnicott, cited in Giovacchini 1990, p.6).

## Theory of play

In 1971, the year of his death, Winnicott's book *Playing and Reality* was published. This collection of essays gives us Winnicott's final thoughts on the significance and meaning of play, a phenomenon that he considered as being universal. Yet sadly, and perhaps as a final paradox, Winnicott died before it was printed. The central thesis of his book is summarised in the following statement in which Winnicott himself tells us 'it is in playing and only in playing that the individual child or adult is able to be creative and to use the whole personality, and it is only in being creative that the individual discovers the self' (2008, p.73).

As ever, Winnicott begins his theoretical statement by making a connection between play and the analytic relationship, telling us that 'psychotherapy tales place in the overlap of two areas of playing, that of the patient and that of the therapist. Psychotherapy has to do with two people playing' (2008, p.51). But in distinguishing his own understanding of play from that of Klein's, Winnicott is quick to make a distinction. He suggests that Klein's psychoanalysis of children was more concerned with the content of play, rather than the playing child as a whole. And returning momentarily to his interest in the music of words he continues by making a distinction between the noun 'play' and the verbal noun 'playing', suggesting that we can expect to find playing just as evident in adult analysis through a patient's choice of words, as in that of children. Having commenced his discourse on the ins and outs of play, so to speak, he reaches the point where in wishing to emphasise the importance of play he pauses, suggesting that he would like to 'set this up the other way round' (2008, p.56). Making one of his definitive statements Winnicott tells us that 'it is play that is universal' (p.56). And listing a number of its benefits, which include that 'play belongs to health, that it leads into group relations, that it is a kind of communication in psychotherapy', he concludes by telling us that psychoanalysis itself 'has been developed as a highly specialised form of playing in the service of communication with oneself and others' (2008, p.56). Adding emphasis to his belief in the playing quality of psychoanalysis, and believing that the 'natural thing is play', Winnicott suggests that psychoanalysis is in fact a twentieth-century version. And it is this concept, that is play, which as a music therapist seems to be at the very core of our particular kind of therapeutic practice, that I now wish to consider.

The developmental processes which happen in the early stages of a baby's life and which go toward forming the foundations upon which he learns to play, happen between mother and baby in a 'to and fro' sort of way. There has to be a kind of marriage between the 'omnipotence of intrapsychic processes with the baby's control of the actual' (2008, p.63) and once he has become confident in his mother's management of this particular dance, an intermediate playground begins to form. The creation of this first playground requires a delicate balance to be maintained, which, as Winnicott suggests, is something akin to magic! And in keeping with the theme of this particular chapter, I would like to beg the reader's indulgence while I play with this particular image, that of magic.

I begin by setting the scene in which my playing will take place. We are in a circus and we can see the audience perched upon the edge of their seats with excitement and in a state of anticipation as the clown makes his entrance holding a bucket. He makes as if to show his audience its content, which they believe could be water but hope that is is not. The clown lifts his bucket, which really contains pieces of paper, and prepares to throw it over the audience. In this very moment, the delicate process of integrating external and internal reality becomes enacted. The audience has been led into accepting the illusion that water is in the bucket, whilst at the same time as believing or hoping that it is not. Arising from crucial elements endemic in the clown's performance the magic is happening. Once the truth is out and the audience is not really soaked (unless of course the clown is sadistic) the mutual playfulness between audience and performer is allowed to evolve and, as a result, trust in the clown's ability to create a mutual playing space affirmed. Throughout this kind of play, keeping a balance between internal states of mind, which for the audience might involve fear and anxiety, with the reality of the external world, must inevitably produce a particular kind of tension. And it is this particular quality of energy that Winnicott understood as driving the activity of play forward. For a mother with her baby, presenting him with what he desires or needs allows him to feel he has created it. So, like the audience who no doubt willed there to be no water in the clown's bucket, and were proven to be right, if all goes well our baby too can begin to believe in a space for playing. As that which he experiences is continually being matched with that which is actually being delivered, an infant can imagine that his wish is her command.

The 'to and fro' quality of this early form of mothering provides the developmental building blocks upon which a baby can develop his sense of healthy omnipotence. This carefully and sensitively attuned process delivered by a mother with her baby, or a clown with his audience, can enable both baby and audience to manage the tension between what is real and external, with that which comes from feelings and thoughts and is therefore internal. It is the internal states of mind that I am attempting to address in the children and adults I see and it is within the to and fro quality of playing that the beginnings of a music therapy relationship begins.

## Musical play

Playing, in the general sense, is at the heart of making music with a child or adult in a music therapy setting. And, as I have already described, it usually takes the form of what music therapists name clinical improvisation. By tuning into the moment to moment musical expressions of our patients, as music mothers and fathers, we can provide that which is waiting to be found. Simply put, using improvised music and based upon composing music in the moment using whatever instrument feels appropriate, the therapist tunes into and/or resonates with the sounds and general expressions of the other. This may include any vocal expressions, which could even include hiccups, for example, or instrumental sounds actually played by a child or adult. Improvising enables the therapist to provide the musical stepping stones upon which a relationship of trust can begin to develop. However, it may be that the patient chooses not to use the instruments provided and, as with Tim in Chapter 6, decide to play with other objects that may be in the room. Or they can even do nothing at all. In this case a therapist may use their music to connect with gestures related to physical movements, such as breathing, or emotionally through reflecting a mood. A music therapist is able to connect with these behaviours by tuning into such elements as the pitch, the rhythm or the tempo of a patient's various communications, including any random sounds or vocal expressions they may make. Therapy can only begin to happen when there is a trusting relationship. Successful moments of meeting or connecting with another can, for a patient, create the illusion that what has been formed between them and the therapist was already there to be found. Or, in the case of music, there to be heard. In other words, at these times of connection, there will have been a good-enough musical fit.

The musical framework within which musical connections are created is, as I have previously described, primarily built upon the element of tempo. Tempo, as denoted by its name, is an element which involves movement, one instant to another. In Winnicott's theory of early development, the element of time has an emotional as well as functional component, and an understanding of this aspect of life is one that a baby has to be supported to develop. In a musical relationship tempo can create a holding framework in which the moment to moment musical connections can evolve. The overall musical experience created within these moments is then able to contribute to the ongoing experience of being met, thus creating in the patient a sense of ongoing-ness, or, in a musical relationship, an ongoing musical-ness. This in turn can contribute to the building up of a sense of reliability in the therapist, which in turn enables a potential space for playing to develop. In this mutually created space, a child or adult can begin to experience more of who they are and, as the therapy evolves, who they are becoming. An example of this process can be seen in the following moment taken from clinical work with a three-and-a-half-year-old girl.

## Susan

Ahead of me runs Susan, a pretty, lively little girl. She flings open the door of the music therapy room, enters and heads straight for the piano. She bangs her forearms down onto the keys, creating a cacophony of crushed notes. A moment's indecision arises, providing a brief pause in which I become aware of the conflict arising in me between accompanying Susan on the piano or playing a different instrument. My split-second response is to shift my physical position at the piano slightly and, moving sideways, stand by the cymbal that is next to it. I hit two slow beats and, for a moment, it feels as if we are playing together. Susan continues on the piano for a few seconds more. She suddenly stops and turning from the keyboard moves toward the metallophone which is placed on the floor, and picks up a beater. She hits several bars individually and I respond by singing 'hallo' in the key suggested by the notes she has just played. I expand upon these particular sounds, improvising a short melody. But as quickly as we begin our second piece of music, Susan ends it and, dropping the beaters, dances away from me over towards the other side of the room. This interaction has taken place in a very short space of time – to be precise, a few seconds.

Susan has a diagnosis of autism and, reflecting on my overall musical experiences with her, I became aware of feeling that an emerging pattern of relating was occurring. This pattern involved us in making a musical connection in which Susan would 'come to life' followed by an immediate or sudden break in contact. In this particular instant, this rupture to our togetherness occurred when Susan literally danced away across the room. Reflecting upon the very first moments of this session, I became aware of another aspect of Susan's behaviour. At the beginning, my instantaneous decision to change direction, both physically and musically, happened in a very short space of time, a split second, yet an instant in which time appeared to stand still. In my experience, often the ways in which someone with autism may behave can evoke the feeling that one needs to be intensely aware of the moment to moment ways in which contact is made, as by doing so it becomes possible to acknowledge and respect the fragility of the other's psychic skin. One needs to be tuned to the fact that a therapist's music may happen too soon, or too quickly, or in too close a proximity, causing someone like Susan to experience a feeling of painful intrusion. In my very first moments together with Susan, in which I was initially sharing both her musical and physical space, I had begun to feel that I was not in the 'right' place or space. Despite the fact that Susan's initial piano chords had created the feeling of a musical 'announcement', and her pauses had created a possible invitation to join her, there was clearly another element present, one could say happening between or perhaps behind the more obvious external musical expressions. The quality of the music created between us in that first instant allowed me to experience something of what could be named as Susan's inner music and therefore something of her understanding and experience of the world. Choosing to play in the way I did allowed Susan to be in a space that she had created, rather than one I had decided to join, enabling me to fine tune to the way in which Susan wished or desired to be connected to me. By meeting Susan on her musical terms, albeit briefly and following these initial moments, it made it possible for us to have an instant of real play together.

Being a successful clown or magician and, I would suggest, also a successful enough therapist, means that you need to have a capacity for developing an intimate and finely tuned relationship between yourself and the audience or, in the case of therapy, between you and your patient. In order for the tricks performed by the clown or the magic to appear as magic, the observer or other must come willingly into their world. Winnicott was careful to point out that, as the opposite of play is coercion, if the analyst becomes dogmatic in any way, playing ceases. So I would suggest that it is possible that playing *our* music may only serve to prevent a child or adult from playing, and can force them to fit in with what we offer.

Relating in a therapeutic relationship, as Khan explains, requires a capacity on behalf of the patient and therapist to 'sustain illusion and to work with it', explaining that the vehicle for working with illusion is 'symbolic discourse', which in psychoanalysis is commonly referred to as being free association. Khan goes on to suggest that if the ability to sustain illusion breaks down then, as he describes, 'the usage of the word has to yield to other forms and styles of relating and experiencing' (1986, p.252). Here perhaps we find the place of such a medium as music. The free associations of verbal therapy become the musical interpretations of a patient's musical gestures.

## Play or playing

In describing how one executes the medium of music, it is usual to adopt the term play or playing. However, believing that someone is actually playing music is not as straightforward as it appears. And, as I would suggest, it is possible for a music therapist to confuse the nature of making music with the act of playing. In order to make a musical sound one has to actually 'play' the instrument. A variety of sounds are consequently created which may be understood as representing aspects of our patient's musical personality. The fact that a child or adult has produced what we might name as being music, can seduce us into believing that our patient is playing. But, if we are to understand Winnicott's particular explanation of this activity, then we may discover that, for some patients, an ability to play in a healthy way may actually be inhibited and what they are doing is something which is not happening in a mutually shared space. Being unable to truly play may be linked to an inability for symbolic thought. In this case, as Winnicott advises, it is the main task of the therapist to enable a patient to play.

This must be done as he suggests, before any therapeutic interpretation can occur. An example of this process took place in music therapy with Simon, an intelligent young man of 26.

## Simon

Simon had been attending music therapy for three months and had been diagnosed with schizophrenia. Following a short admission he was now attending as a day patient. Simon had requested music therapy in order, as he explained, to 'improve his communication and express his anger'. Simon described that he had once been in a band playing the drums but that he had preferred to play them melodically, recalling that on occasion he had even followed the vocals. Simon's music, which was often played on the piano, was extremely difficult to listen to and at times even unbearable. And any ability on my part to make sense of the music became immediately annihilated.

Following one of our many musical pieces in which we played together, Simon described it as being 'good'. As this had not been my experience, it was difficult to understand what this might mean. In fact, throughout the whole time of our playing, I had felt as if I had been trapped in a musical tunnel of chaotic and fragmented sounds and one that seemed to go on forever. On later reflection, and taking into consideration other comments Simon had made, it seemed as if he was experiencing life as back to front or in reverse. What I mean by this is that by describing the unbearable quality of our music together as 'good' and his previous drum playing as melodic, good had become bad, rhythm had become melody and, from another later comment, looking became touching.

A psychotic state of mind is one in which sense can be turned into non-sense and objects are turned around, engendering a world of chaos and strange meaning. Simon often used a lot of words to try and describe his ideas and feelings. Yet, despite this ability, it was not always easy to understand his meaning. From an external observer's point of view it was clear to see that we were actually playing music together. Yet the overwhelming quality of Simon's music made it impossible for me to feel that we were involved in shared play. I felt continually drowned out, and involved in an ongoing musical nightmare. Equally, it became clear that Simon appeared unable to hold a sense of me as an other alive object in his mind. This became vividly demonstrated in his response to the holiday breaks. Just before a particularly long break, and after I had explained when we would next meet, Simon responded by being surprised that our sessions would be continuing. In his mind, it appeared that my temporary disappearance had become equated with my total disappearance. So that out of sight would literally mean out of mind and forever.

As Winnicott's understanding of play links to how we come to make sense of our world, as well as being a particular form of communication, an ability to play is one which helps us to grasp a sense of reality. Hannah Segal describes that 'play is a way both of exploring reality and of mastering it... It is also learning to distinguish between the symbolic and the real' (2003, p.211).

It was clear that Simon could allow himself to explore the musical environment. Yet his capacity for symbolic thought, the 'as if' of life, appeared inhibited and his understanding of the world described in concrete meaningless terms. Susan Sontag (1976, p.20) describes a particular quality of speech which she defines as being dissociated. She writes, 'speech dissociated from the body (and therefore from feeling), speech not organically informed by the sensuous presence... becomes false, inane, ignoble, weightless'. It would seem that Simon was yet to discover the relationship between his thoughts, his fantasies and external reality. For now, the most important aspect of our relationship was my ability to provide an environment in which Simon could be brought gently into a place where our musical connections were allowed to become meaningful and where playing could begin without fear of annihilation.

When offering music therapy, the question as to whether a child or adult is able to play in a Winnicottian sense is one which I believe must be held in mind. It is easy to believe through our patients' musical expressions that they are really playing. The split-second moments in Susan's therapy for example, were those in which I could feel connected or disconnected in every sense of the word. Allowing myself to go with the experience that my primitive musical self evoked, rather than with what was apparent, took Susan and me to a place, albeit for only a short while, in which we came together and were able to play. In contrast, Simon's persecuted state of mind needed a space to be heard and literally held. Any interpretation of his words only served to confuse him. If play is, as Winnicott tells us, 'always on the theoretical line between the subjective and that which is objectively perceived' (2008, p.68) and the patient's sense of reality is precarious, then playing in its Winnicottian sense cannot be done. As therapists we are, as Winnicott tells us, 'reaching for the child's [adult's] communication' (2008, p.53). To summarise, and using words from Phillips, 'playing is the process of finding through pleasure what interests you, but it is by definition a state of transitional knowing, creative by virtue of being always inconclusive.' He concludes, 'and, of course, though there is word-play, playing is not exclusively verbal' (1988, p.144).

# CHAPTER 9

# A Sense of Self and Music Therapy

*Feeling real is more than existing; it is finding a way to exist as oneself, and to relate to objects as oneself, and to have a self into which to retreat for relaxation.*

(Winnicott 2008, p.158)

We can occasionally find ourselves being asked to describe who we are, whether for a job application, for example, or at a party where we are engaging with people we do not know. But in whatever circumstances we find ourselves answering this question, we may well come up with several quite different replies.

When Winnicott came onto the psychoanalytic scene he began to use the term 'self', and, as Phillips tells us, in 'an idiosyncratic and sometimes mystifying way' (1988, p.3) which was not necessarily in keeping with psychoanalytic theory. In his own words Winnicott writes about the self thus: 'A word like 'self' naturally knows more than we do; it uses us, and can command us' (Winnicott 1990, p.158). The poetry of this statement brings into focus a concept which for Winnicott was connected to our ability to feel alive. Working with babies and their mothers for most of his life, he was regularly placed in a position in which he could wonder about the kind of self that he observed developing. In fact, at one point in his paper 'The Theory of Parent–Infant Relationship' (1960) Winnicott refers to what he names as being the 'core of the personality' and, as if assuming that we understand this term, moves quickly on to talk about the 'concept of the true self'. But what does it mean to have a self? In what ways does this self we discover become represented internally?

Beginning with Winnicott's famous or infamous statement that there is no such thing as a baby, only a mother and a baby, we have a picture of a system co-created by two individuals. It was Winnicott's deep belief that an essential part of a mother's role was to protect the infant self so that he could be led toward becoming a person who is available for others. A mother's protection is necessary because at the very beginning of life, as Winnicott explains, 'there is not sufficient ego strength for there to be a reaction without loss of identity' (Winnicott 1992, p.182).

In his early state of vulnerability an infant may be easily disturbed by aspects of early life. If helped to manage the feelings which arise, then certain disturbances can be healthy, but beyond a certain degree can 'bring about a reaction'. Always careful in his use of terminology, by using the term 'react', Winnicott highlights the qualitative difference between this and the word 'respond'. For if an infant has not been helped to manage the rough and tumble life brings, then it is also possible for there to be a 'capacity for false and unhealthy forward movement in emotional development' (p.182).

Always able to acknowledge the learning he received from his patients, Winnicott uses material arising during one of his patient's treatments in order to illustrate his point, which, as he explains, was 'worked out' during analysis. The strength of the image painted by his patient gives the reader a real feeling for how a particular difficult early state of being might be received by an infant. To place her experience in context, this patient's own early environment was infused with feelings created by a mother who was depressed and who, in her distress, would hold her infant 'tightly for fear of dropping her' (p.182). I think it is important to quote the description in full. Winnicott writes:

> At the beginning the individual is like a bubble. If the pressure from outside actively adapts to the pressure within, then the bubble is the significant thing, that is to say the infant's self. If, however, the environmental pressure is greater or less than the pressure within the bubble, then it is not the bubble that is important but the environment. The bubble starts to adapt to the outside pressure. (p.183)

As in this patient's case, a Winnicottian baby will have pre-birth as well as post-natal experiences of its environment, which for various reasons may force the baby to react. Being placed in a position of having to react at a time when the ego is yet to be fully formed means that a potential 'state of being' is disturbed. This is not a conducive environmental condition for the 'true self' to emerge. In fact, and introducing us to his second term, it can force the baby into creating a 'false self'. The function of this 'false self' is to hide the true self 'until a sufficiently nurturing environment can be found in which development can start up again'. In Winnicott's own words, 'the False Self has as its main concern a search for conditions which will make it possible for the True Self to come into its own' (Winnicott 1992, p.143).

We become who we are in the beginning through metabolising, as it were, a sense of a self, building it from all the cues, expressions, gestures and overall handling our primary care giver, usually our mother, has carried out with us. The external management of our care involves a constant current of emotional charge, the shaping of which we eventually internalise, forming the clay of our relational experiences of self into a management of a self, a me with a me. Bollas suggests that 'our handling of our self as an object partly inherits and expresses the history of our experience as the parental object' (Bollas 1991, p.51). We become who we are through the ways in which we have been cared for, which includes the parental 'forms of self perception, self facilitation, self handling and self refusal' (p.51).

Later in our lives we come to represent aspects of this 'historical theatre' in how we manage parts of our self and in the ways we treat our self as an object. Freud evolved the term superego to describe the voice which 'objectifies' part of our self in order to think. And we are, as it were, for ever having conversations with ourselves in order to manage how we function in the world. Aspects of these conversations represent an internalised model of relating, which may have included unhelpful ways of being, and ones that do not support us to function in a healthy way.

## Paul

From the minute four-year-old Paul entered the room he began his conversation with himself. His self-language was of his own making and therefore not of the external world into which he had stepped. His spoken sounds appeared to guide him around the room in such a way that it seemed as if he were in bubble of his own. Amongst his sounds it was possible to distinguish specific words which appeared to have a communicative intention, yet Paul's utterances were not symbols formed by a shareable language. Equally the absorption within his own world was not total, as Paul diligently kept watch upon me whilst tiptoeing around the room. Only when he needed to manage his feelings arising from the impingement of the external musical environment did his language become recognisable and one to which I could respond. My initial playing of the piano as an introductory relational framework to the session was clearly intrusive, causing Paul to find words of a shared language that I would understand and hopefully act upon. His instruction for me to 'stop' had the desired effect and my music and the potential shared musical sound world ceased. In this moment I became a music mother with no useful resources.

As babies we absorb and internalise the processes of mothering with all its dynamics, its nuances of expression and the musical elements of relating, assimilating and shaping our experiences into patterns of relating. Our sense of a self is dependent upon both what and how we experience the external world, followed by what these experiences come to mean.

When our sense of a self is still forming, our experiences of care are stored in various ways within our system. One of the areas in which this happens is within in our bodies and as a result, as Bollas suggests, 'this body memory conveys memories of our early existence' (Bollas 1991, p.46). We are as one and all that effects us when we are totally dependent and completely vulnerable, affects our whole being. If, as is often the case that traumatic experiences occur in early life, then 'the psyche is…unable to process it and is liable to store trauma in body memory… The patient's body has had to share the burden… with the psyche' (Solomon 2004, p.649). In my next clinical example we observe the ways in which Andrew's bodily expressions reveal aspects of his internalised model of care. We are able to see how they become expressed through his ways of relating to the objects within the music therapy environment.

## Andrew

Three-and-a-half-year-old Andrew threw himself into the music therapy room. Landing on the floor, he lifted up the cabassa and, in an attempt to play it, sent it spinning across the room. Picking himself up, Andrew started to move over to where the cabassa had landed and in so doing, fell over another much larger instrument which was in his pathway. The fall appeared to send Andrew in another direction and toward the piano, against which was leaning a guitar. Standing next to it was a cymbal blocking its access. Rather than go around behind the instruments, Andrew attempted to squeeze himself into a small gap between them both, resulting in a potential catastrophe, averted only by my intervention. Our first few minutes of therapy together left me feeling as if I had entered a war zone, in which the unpredictability of the environment, together with the possibility of an imminent catastrophe, created an atmosphere of potential disaster.

Through her care, a mother is continuously acquainting her infant's body and psyche one with each other. And according to how she manages this process her infant's sense of a self will come about. But at times, and as Winnicott suggests, this process of integration may not happen. As a result, a degree of dissociation may occur between body and mind. Andrew's historical ambivalent relationship with his parents had in part become memorised in a body memory and expressed through his bodily management of himself. His occupation of the physical space had appeared awkward and at odds with its content through his external actions. My own responses to Andrew arose from his unconscious projected elements of his internalised model of maternal care, causing me to become intensely anxious. As the session moved on I began to experience increasing feelings of overwhelming danger, as if at any moment something calamitous might occur. In these moments, Andrew's chaotic and un-held quality of maternal care became vividly represented within the music therapy environment and his sense of self in relation to the external world of objects appeared to be one in which he was unable to differentiate between where his bodily self ended and where the external world began. The impact of Andrew's early experiences had clearly caused him to struggle to be able to find a self in which he could feel safely held. This made it difficult for him to have a mental space in which he could be come curious about the world.

Many years earlier than Solomon's reference to a body memory, Winnicott produced a paper entitled 'Basis for the Self in Body' (1970). In referring to his previous idea of depersonalisation, a term Winnicott used to describe a child or a patient's 'loss of contact with the body and body functioning', he tells us that 'the basis of a self forms on the fact of the body, which being alive, not only has its shape, but which also functions' (Winnicott *et al.* 1989, p.270). For Andrew, his internalised process of care had absorbed aspects of his parents' own internalised relational models of attachment, which had been equally unpredictable and inconsistent. His sense of a self, therefore, had become formed out of a pattern of care which had created an anxious and un-held self and one which, as a result, created feelings of intense ambivalence whenever an opportunity for self-exploration presented itself. For a child to be able to develop a curiosity about the world of objects, he has to 'be seen for what he (is) at any moment'. Only then can he 'afford to look and see'. It is therefore a mother's 'active presence, her deep instruction, her activities as a transformational object, that the baby integrates into the psyche structure that constitutes the ego; in this grammar of the ego are stored the rules for handling of the self and the objects' (Bollas 1991, p.60).

Gaining a sense of a self is a process which happens in various ways and most significantly, as Winnicott believed, through a mother's role which is 'giving back to the baby the baby's own self'. What the baby sees when he looks at his mother's face is himself. She is the human mirror into which he gazes and which helps him build a sense of self in which he is able learns to know how he feels. Should his mother be preoccupied, then the mirror will show the feelings of his mother and he will be unable to find himself. 'He looks and does *not* see himself, but the mother's face. The mother's face is not then a mirror' (Winnicott 2008, p.151).

## Dawn

Sitting in the baby group was Dawn. Beside her was Leo, her eight-month-old baby boy. We are all getting ready to sing and play the hallo music which defines the start of the group and will bring everyone into readiness. Dawn has not been sleeping well and is tired and feeling depressed. She appears overwhelmed by Leo and is clearly finding it difficult to engage with him. Dawn picks Leo up and in readiness for our first song rests him on her lap facing her. The music begins and as we reach the point where each mother sings the name of her baby, Dawn is struggling. Although she is looking at Leo and singing his name, something about the timbre of her voice does not appear to engage him. Leo's response is to squirm and turn his body away from his mother's face. He fixes his gaze upon the mother sitting nearby and in response Dawn appears to mirror Leo's reaction, also turning herself away from him and looking in a different direction. The pain of their mismatch is palpable and something which as the session progresses, we as 'grand-mothering therapists' are there to gently address. Dawn's own struggles in that moment had been too much for Leo to bear. When he looked at his mother, all he could see was her own feelings of ambivalence. There was no space and no place for Leo or a Leo self.

As Winnicott explains, 'the mother who is not good enough is not able to implement the infant's omnipotence, and so she repeatedly fails to meet the infant; instead she substitutes her own gesture which is to be given sense by the compliance of the infant. This compliance is the earliest stage of the False Self' (1990, p.145). Leo's mother had found herself in a painful and difficult place. She needed to be held and supported by us as therapists and her feelings acknowledged, in order that she could begin to feel good enough for her little boy.

In a paper entitled 'Reparation in Respect of Mother's Organised Defence against Depression' (1948) we learn that depression is something which could 'sabotage' an infant's development. A mother suffering from this state of mind can only take care of her own mood and to the cost of her infant's own needs. In order to survive, infants such as Leo will have to fit in with their mother's moods. They become compliant. As a baby they are compelled to 'study the variable maternal visage in an attempt to predict the mother's mood, just exactly as we all study the weather' (Winnicott 2008, p.152). Phillips tells us that Winnicott is proposing that 'the lively child with a depressed mother is having to sustain the mother's vitality'(1988, p.92). He finds himself having to take on his mother's depression which leads him to becoming identified with her state of being. This forces him into complying with his mother's needs. His own needs therefore become subservient and his way of life becomes reactive.

As with many of Winnicott's thinking about the early relationship, there are analogies between this and the psychoanalytic connection. Providing her baby with an experience of being held in mind is an essential part of the mothering process. It is the process which eventually leads to the development of a mind in her baby which he can then use in order that he can come to understand his own self and others. As part of development in early care and in the therapeutic relationship, a mother with her baby or a therapist with their patient can allow them to know that they have been thought about and there are many ways in which this can be achieved. Through facial, vocal, or gestural expressions and, in a music therapy relationship particularly, in the overall music co-created by the therapist through moment to moment experiences that are framed in time and space. Out of this relational dance a baby or patient is able to have a sense that they have been held in mind.

As therapists it is essential to present our patients with a thinking mind. So that they can feel they are not alone in the historical narrative of their original object relationships, as outsiders we must be able to hold a place for our patients which is not contaminated by elements of the original story. In music therapy we enter the patient's world through direct musical exchanges, reflections and expressions which evolve as the relationship progresses. Just as the baby needs to know that his mother can think about how things are, so as therapists, and acting as the third external object to the patient's internalised model of relating we must be willing to find ways of creating spaces with our patients where we are able to think about and reflect upon their experiences. This is never more necessary than with someone who has a diagnosis of autism and for whom the world is a strange and sometimes alien place.

## Daisy

Daisy expressed herself physically, often skipping about the room in a dance-like fashion. On this occasion I began to follow her dance with my piano music. I kept pace with her lilting tempo of movement, shaping her dance with musical phrasing and emphasis. As the musical dance continued, Daisy ran to and fro, back and forward from the door to the corner of the room until she threw herself down onto the floor, landing beside a metallophone. She picked up the beaters and began to hit the notes. Matching her sounds, I played in the same key, and in this moment I am literally and directly able to tune into Daisy's notes and, more significantly, into the musicality of her aliveness. We make music together for nearly a minute before Daisy breaks away and moves off in another direction and into another world.

Working with those for whom gathering a coherent historical narrative is difficult and who come with a diagnosis of psychosis forces us to really question the meaning of life or, as Winnicott put it, 'what life itself is about' (Winnicott 2008, p.133). As therapists we know that good-enough early experiences cannot be taken for granted and there are those for whom their early holding environment has failed. This can lead to a depleted internal state in which it feels as if they have 'not started to exist'. Their lives become 'characterised by a sense of futility' (Phillips 1988, p.127). In the case of psychoanalysis and in music therapy, we need to provide the kind of environment in which, as Winnicott writes, 'the patient will find his or her own self, and will be able to exist and to feel real' (Winnicott 2008, p.158). For someone like Daisy, the difficulties encountered in her continual struggles to find and connect with another, reflected a 'yet to be formed self'. There was a sense in which the feet of this dancing little girl appeared to never touch the floor and the elusive and delicate quality of her being made it difficult to hold her. But after many months of *lifeless* musical play, quite unexpectantly a moment of aliveness arrived. In that moment our shared music had been filled with intense feeling created not through imitation but, as Stern would say, through a space in which 'attunement' could happen. As my musical interpretations and elaborations of Daisy's movements evolved, a thinking space began to form. And one in which I was able to hold a Daisy self. Through the music we had created together, we had been able to have a musical experience which was alive and one that had allowed Daisy to discover a self who could be with an other.

In a therapeutic relationship our patients bring us what we need to know and, in the simplest terms, the essence of this kind of relationship is as Winnicott tells us, by and large 'a long term giving the patient back what the patient brings' (Winnicott 2008, p.158). In music therapy we see children and adults with a range of early environmental experiences and who may therefore be affected in significantly different ways. Continually making links between the earliest relationship and the practice of psychoanalysis, Winnicott refers to the different kinds of patients that we might see. Broadly, he appears to understand them as presenting in two ways. First those we could name as being the more ordinary neurotic patient, in whom we understand there to be a sense of 'ongoing continuity of self,' and reflecting the existence of a good-enough mother. Second, we may see a child or adult who has more disturbed personal qualities and who is therefore 'in danger of disintegrating at the slightest hint of failure in the holding environment'. In this case, the person's own self has become the problem...' (Wright 1998, p.3). Ultimately, a patient needs 'to be known in all his bits and pieces by one person the analyst' (Winnicott 1992, p.150). The task of the infant, and one could say of the therapist therefore, is to provide an adult or child within the therapeutic setting with an opportunity of integrating his self. As in the initial quote and, as Winnicott explains, 'I like to think of my work this way, and to think that if I do this well enough the patient will find his or her own self, and will be able to exist and to feel real' (Winnicott 2008, p.158).

# CHAPTER 10

# Transference and Countertransference

*What is* [music] *therapy? It is essentially a conversation which involves listening to and* playing *with those in trouble with the aim of helping them understand and resolve their predicament.*

(Brown and Pedder 1991, p.xi, modified)

As you can see, I have begun this chapter with a straightforward quote, originally about psychotherapy and altered in order to introduce this chapter on the specific therapeutic tools of transference and countertransference. So let us go immediately to the music therapy room where five-year-old Mia is about to begin her first session of music therapy.

## Mia

As Mia had already been attending nursery and had therefore been used to being separated from her mother, following a discussion with both mother and Mia together, it was decided that she could attend music therapy on her own. From the beginning of our time together, Mia's curiosity and interest in the musical environment led her to explore the setting. But suddenly, and as if catching herself unawares, Mia began to cry. My response was to stop the music I had begun to play on the piano and verbally try to reassure her. As I was speaking, I began to realise that the quality of my voice was unusually high and sing song in timbre. In fact it was a voice I did not recognise. Later in the session, and following the introduction of mother into the therapeutic space, as Mia played she began to accompany her musical expressions verbally, alternating between praising her and checking her behaviour. It was then that I recognised the voice I had heard coming from myself earlier. Evoked by Mia's enactment of her internalised experiences of mothering, the unconsciously expressed quality of my verbal intervention had taken on qualities of Mia's mother's verbal expressions.

In the early moments of our therapeutic relationship, Mia had unconsciously recreated and transferred relational aspects of her own mothering process into the therapeutic setting. This we call a transference phenomena. Arising from the feelings I subsequently experienced and which had been projected into me, I had momentarily taken on aspects of her early care, reacting to and talking with Mia in a tone of voice which would have been more appropriate for a much younger child. These qualities had become manifest in the embodied musical nuances of my voice and subsequently my vocal interventions. This phenomenon we name countertransference and, in particular, projective identification. Through tuning into Mia's ambivalent distress, I had entered into a shared experience of her inner world, which as Woodhead tells us, forms a 'joint (but not mutual) history that is unique (to them)' (Woodhead 2004, p.147).

In this clinical example I have introduced the two phenomena which are at the core of a therapeutic relationship and which, if understood, can provide a therapist with essential information about his patient. The mothering object defined within the transference relationship will not be a truly rounded representation. In fact Bollas suggests that we can only grasp a patient's psychic reality in part for, as he tells us, its logic is 'more akin to the nature of poetry and music than to abstract thought or, the secondary process' (1993, p.109). The ways in which a patient expresses elements of their mothering object within the therapeutic setting will provide manifestations of early care and, if permitted, will be revealed through the patient's use of the whole therapeutic setting. As we know, a developing baby integrates qualities of his mother's 'active presence', and will absorb the ways in which he has been handled, which includes holding. His experience of these two aspects of the mothering process will then come to define how he will use others 'as his objects (ordinary transference) and then, how he relates to and handles himself as an object (transference and countertransference)' (Bollas 1993, p.60) in everyday life. It is Bollas's belief that 'each person transfers elements of the parents' child care to his own handling of himself as an object' (p.59), so that as well as to others, there is also transference to our self as an object. These transference phenomena Bollas divides into what he terms as the 'inherited (true self) and the environmental' (p.59).

For Mia, it was her initial handling of herself in the room with me that provoked her distress. Her desire to explore the musical environment led to a developing internal conflict, revealing itself as a state of being torn between the new and interesting music mother environment and his original mother object. The musical world of objects had been initially attractive to Mia, but her curiosity had quickly become connected to feelings of insecurity. Finding myself comforting Mia was my response to the projected feelings of an insecure baby, and one who had yet to feel securely attached enough to be independent from his original mother object. As Bollas describes, if a child does not have experience of a holding environment, then they will 'feel hesitant to release the elements of self to their experiencings: such abandonments feel life threatening' (Bollas 1993, p.53).

Part of a therapeutic task is 'to determine what figure he (therapist) represents for the patient at any given moment whilst trying to retain his knowledge of who he is for himself' (Hinshelwood 1991, p.44). This is an ever-moving process and one which the tools of transference and countertransference can facilitate. Through awareness of their impact, the information they can reveal will enable a therapist to experience for himself elements of the patient's inner world.

In a musical exchange, I believe that the impact of these two phenomena can be intensely powerful, as the directness of the musical language appears to bypass ordinary defences, allowing a child or adult's feelings to lodge themselves bodily and psychologically within the therapist. The non-verbal language of music permits the pre-verbal elements of a patient's inner world to enter our being, bringing primitive aspects of a patient's early care into focus. Often, only when we are away from the therapeutic setting and out of range, so to speak, of a patient's projections can our understanding become clear.

Transference is a word that can be used in an ordinary way, and describes the ways in which others may come to represent our early parental figures, for example a new boss or the bank manager. Historically, in the early psychoanalytic world, Klein viewed psychoanalysis and therefore the transference in classical terms, meaning that the therapist was 'relatively anonymous in her account' (Phillips 1988, p.91). It was sometime before countertransference became recognised. In fact Freud considered it to be 'the neurotic transference of the analyst to the patient', and required that 'it be eliminated by the analyst's self-control' (Hinshelwood 2002, p.42).

The early idea of the 'blank canvas' approach to analysis, whereby the analyst would behave in an almost mechanical way, was eventually discarded, as the realisation that analysts were experiencing emotional responses to their patients grew. Analysts, particularly those considering themselves as being of the Independent School of thinking, recognised the interactive nature of the transference and countertransference phenomena and in describing its development from 1950, Heimann wrote, 'the analyst's emotional response to his patient within the analytic situation represents one of the most important tools for his work. The analyst's counter-transference is an instrument into the patient's unconscious' (1950, p.31).

Joseph (1985) considered that the therapeutic experience is a 'total transference activity, where everything from moment to moment, is part of the transference and countertransference'. And Cox believed that these phenomena cannot exist without each other. He explains:

> The transferring of feelings, drives and attitudes from the there-and-then to the here-and-now (and *vice versa*), invested in the therapist by the patient, constitutes transference, and, *per contra*, those invested in the patient by the therapist, constitutes countertransference. (1978, p.120)

Winnicott's clinical observations and practice with children and their families strongly influenced the ways in which he created the framework within which his work as a psychoanalyst was carried out. His understanding of the early mother–infant relationship influenced the development of the therapeutic perimeters and the conditions within which he believed a patient could express elements of their early environment. He linked this early mother–infant environment with the analytic relationship, understanding such aspects as mother/analyst reliability and the mother/analyst adaptation to her baby/patient as being essential components of the therapeutic setting. In appreciating this kind of relationship as being a metaphor for the early mother–infant dyad, Winnicott considered that one of the aims of therapy was to address the point in a patient's life at which the environment had failed. He believed that this could happen if the therapist is 'prepared to follow the patient's unconscious process' and, almost as a word of warning adds, 'if he is not to issue a directive and so step outside the analyst's role' (Winnicott 1992, p.297).

For Winnicott, the baby who has had to live as if there is no mother, or in other words has found himself only able to fit in with his mother's needs, is incapable of modifying his early environment and the grievance becomes 'turned against the self' (Phillips 1988, p.96). Therefore, in Winnicottian terms, one of the aims of analysis would be 'to help the patient sort out environmental failure from that which he can genuinely take responsibility for as a part of himself' (Phillips 1988, p.96).

Bollas underscores Winnicott's thinking, proposing that the appearance of early environmental elements in the transference occur as patients experience the analyst as what he names as being an 'environment–mother'. This experience is, he believes, to be one connected to pre-verbal memories and therefore, as he suggests, has no words. What is needed, he proposes, is 'unintrusive holding' involving an empathic mode of communication.

Bollas may not agree, but perhaps this is exactly where music as a therapeutic language can literally come into play.

In Mia's session, and later on, a moment of 'unintrusive holding' emerged, when having wormed her way past me to the top end of the piano, we found ourselves playing together in a rhythmically framed piano piece. The rhythmical emphasis facilitated synchronised movements both between us and within our individual bodies, supporting Mia's embodiment of herself. Within the music she therefore experienced indirect or 'unintrusive holding'.

A patient comes to therapy to tell their story. The point of view from which they will reveal their narrative establishes, as Bollas describes, 'crucial aspects of the transferences' as well as 'to the self as object and those countertransferences evoked' (1991, p.61). What the patient may discover as the transference relationship unfolds, if as therapists we do not interfere, are aspects of him self with other. Or, as Bollas puts it, 'the person gradually discovers the private language of self' (1991, p.61).

In Winnicottian therapy, transference in the psychoanalytic setting is the material a patient brings, containing 'samples' of their 'past and inner reality'. When these samples are exposed, they become represented in fantasy within the 'ever-changing relationship to the analyst' (Winnicott 1986, p.103). In Mia's early moments of therapy, she had brought her confused and chaotically mothered self into our relationship. Through exposing the insecure part of her being, she had aroused in me a quality of mothering that included a sense of ambivalence. As a result, I had been prompted into becoming an over-protective therapist.

As well as bringing aspects of the early relationship into the setting, for Winnicott transference is also a tool by which a patient brings 'innumerable samples of (their) personal conflicts' (1986, p.106) and is a phenomena which allows unconscious aspects of a their psyche to be revealed. This can happen through the various ways in which they will use the therapeutic setting, which as I believe, in music therapy may also include non-musical objects. But even though in our particular setting we might expect the musical elements to be used musically, we may find that the significant aspect of a child or adult's behaviour is not revealed through their actual choice of instrument or musical form of expression. Rather, and more importantly, in how they use them.

Baradon's observations of the mother–infant relationship endorses this aspect of the transference between a baby with its mother and an adult in therapy, emphasising that the imparting of our inner life arises more through how we relate to objects rather than what the object actually is. She concludes that in early development, a baby will internalise a process 'derived from an object'.

Mia's internalised mothering process revealed itself in all the different ways she used the musical objects, which naturally included me as therapist: the banging together of one instrument upon another in baby-like fashion, the constant tripping over and her awkward physical movements arising from her inability to hold herself together and the instant upset when I began to play the piano. Each of these particular behaviours revealed elements of Mia's internalised early environmental care and therefore an inner sense of herself within it. Arising from how Mia was being with me, I had found myself experiencing strong protective feelings toward both her, as she regularly fell or tripped up, and the music therapy environment, which was variously knocked or banged about. For 'it is with the unconscious child in the patient that the analyst is *most* concerned; and because this child so often treats the analyst as parent, the analyst's unconscious can hardly fail to respond in some degree by regarding the patient as his child' (Money-Kyrle 1989, p.23).

Winnicott's understanding of the early mother–infant environmental set-up led him to view the traditional approach to transference phenomena adopted by the Freudian and then Kleinian orientated therapists, as one which raised several questions in his mind. Such as: 'What was the analyst's desire *vis à vis* the patient, what was the analyst using the patient for, how did the patient figure in the analyst's developmental project?' (Phillips 1988, p.91). For Winnicott, it was equally important to consider the effect a mother's depression could have upon her infant, than to treat the infant alone. 'After all, in the mother–infant couple there was always an overlap of two sets of developmental needs, it was not only the infant who was developing' (Phillips 1988, p.91). An example of how this unified development evolves came in my work with mothers and their babies together. This was a music therapy group for those mothers suffering with a diagnosis of depression and having difficulty with forming a positive attachment to their infant.

## Laura

Mother and eight-month-old Laura were sat with each other in a circle of mothers and babies. We were halfway through our music therapy session and had begun one of our action songs, in which a mother gently moves her hand instrument around the arc of her baby's visual periphery. This particular musical play was created in order to encourage mother and baby in playful eye contact. Accompanying the group song on the piano I added my voice, bringing emphasis and amplification to the physical movements as well as to the words of the song. As my voice rose and fell in pitch, in the middle of the song, Laura looked across toward me and held my gaze for a few moments. When the song had finished and there was much chatter and discussion, Laura's mother made a point of turning toward me, making the comment that she thought Laura had taken more notice of my voice than her own. Mother's projected feelings prompted me to feel immediately placed in the position of being a 'better mother', and one who was resourceful. In her own mind mother had transferred and projected her feelings of being a good-enough mother into me, dividing her own resources of being 'good and not good enough' between us. In that moment of connection with Laura and in mother's mind I had contained the good qualities of mothering, thus depleting her of her own sense of goodness. As a therapist it can be easy to fall into the trap of feeling satisfied about having something to offer. And why not? But this comment had arisen from mother's countertransference feelings which had crossed my radar quickly. In the transference, mother's feelings of worthlessness embodied in her were expressed verbally accompanied by a painful nervous giggle. My role as 'grandmusicmother' was to support mother in discovering her own good-enough qualities so that Laura could also find a resourceful mother.

Throughout the short time this episode had occurred, the emotional temperature of the group, and of Laura's mother in particular, had audibly shifted, both literally in the music, and verbally in the discussion. As therapists working with the transference and countertransference feelings, it is important to be able to 'make enough contact with the patient's feelings and thoughts to feel and experience oneself what is going on in the patient' (Hinshelwood 2002, p.45). Opening ourselves to our patient's feelings allows them to convey their distress in a direct way, which may mean that we too become disturbed. But, 'it is necessary that the analyst feel the disturbance, and can thus be said to become disturbed himself' (p.45).

In our therapeutic relationships, whether verbally based or framed in the language of music, we may experience a myriad of musical changes in the moment to moment connections and interactions. Yet as the music of the music and the music of the words created together evolves, so as therapists we are exposed to the atmosphere of a child or adult's inner world, along with their early experiences of their first environment. If we allow ourselves to be truly in the music of therapy in its widest sense, even though we may not always be making music ourselves, then we become open to what Meltzer named as the emotional temperature and distance (1976).

In his collected works he refers to the element of communication, 'intensity of affect', as involving the two aspects of 'emotional temperature' and 'distance'. He writes:

> Its [intensity of affect's] elements would be ordinary ones of music: tone, rhythm, key, volume, and timbre. By modulating these musical elements we can control the emotionality of the voice and thus what I mean by personal communication. This in turn has an impact on the emotional atmosphere of the consulting room and the reverberation between patient and analyst, variously heightening or dampening this atmosphere. (Meltzer 1976/1994, p.63)

Here Meltzer is clearly referring to the use of the voice in traditional psychoanalysis. But in music therapy we are able to experience direct communications through the changing musical nuances of the music created. In my work with Mia the initial 'emotional temperature' arose out of the countertransference feelings, which had allowed me to experience her mother's vocal and therefore emotional interventions. As the session progressed and after mother joined us, the atmosphere changed dramatically, through Mia's response to herself as an object with me and subsequently between me as music mother, mother with Mia and Mia with both of us together.

For this mother and daughter dyad, the continual changes in the emotional musicality of mother's voice from being supportive and light in quality, to admonishing and harsh in timbre, proved confusing for her Mia. Swinging from one emotional temperature to another made for an unpredictable nature to their relationship and a difficulty in Mia's capacity to allow her to be fully curious about her external world. Her fulltime occupation, therefore, was constant vigilance on her mother and a careful barometer check of the constant changes of her mood.

Awareness of transference and countertransference feelings in an ongoing therapeutic relationship can bring us into contact with the dark and isolated places of a patient's psyche and may in consequence affect our capacity to navigate the therapeutic journey. An example of this occurred in my work with Deborah.

## Deborah

Deborah began attending therapy when she lost her grandfather. She was very close to him and particularly because he had come to live with her and her mum during his final days. Deborah had not known her father as he had abandoned his wife whilst she was pregnant with Deborah. Mother and daughter therefore had a particularly tightly knit relationship and one which, as Deborah entered her adolescence, had become more strained. Mother decided that Deborah should come for therapy as she had had several angry outbursts since her grandfather died and was becoming more isolated at home. When she began therapy, in spite of functioning satisfactorily at school, Deborah sat still and silent, looking at me in a challenging way that evoked feelings of expectancy. As the session moved on I began to feel something of the empty and angry feelings held within Deborah and which she had unconsciously projected into me. As weeks went by I became aware of an increase in the intensity of negative feelings arising in me before the start of each session, causing me to dread our forthcoming time together. I quickly realised that Deborah's projected state of mind, in the countertransference, had led me to become disabled in my capacity to think about her, both during our sessions and in the gap between. As a result I found myself in a state of entrapment with nothing to offer. One could say that we were both lost and as Cox describes, walking in the mountains where 'neither can see the summit.' But as he suggests, 'however turbulent the transference, the therapist tries to retain contact with landmarks' (1978, p.56).

Bringing my work into a space in which I could find some thinking, that is supervision, is one way of maintaining an awareness of the 'landmarks'. By accessing my capacity for considering Deborah from a more objective perspective, my frozen state of mind began to melt, releasing me from the tormenting grip of Deborah's equally paralysed state of mind. I was then able to think about the quality of her relationship with her mother and to consider how I could help Deborah to move forward.

Douglas (2007, p.120) refers to the fact that for some children interpretation is not something to which they can respond. Rather what needs to be established first, is as she calls it, 'a responsive object'. In a music therapy relationship, a music mother object can be created directly, meeting the pre-verbal states of being through emotional, physical and cognitive pathways. Discovering that words did not reach Deborah, I moved from verbal language to musical language, suggesting that we play music together. Our first music continued for nearly 25 minutes and without a pause. Initially I chose to improvise around Deborah's repeated pattern of notes, expanding and elaborating her simple sounds. Realising that she was disappearing musically, I honed my music and rather than 'being as a clever musician' tuned down and into the delicate and fragile sounds of Deborah. It was only when it became necessary to end the session that we were able to stop playing. In her description of how she had experienced our musical play, Deborah explained that she had found that she was able to be 'in her own world', which she described as being safe and predictable. Also she was relieved that she did not have to use words. Perhaps the place in which we found ourselves together was one in which the baby part of Deborah had felt held, reminding her of a time when being together with another did not require words. For now, it was enough for us to be in the music, until such time as Deborah felt able to consider her more uncomfortable feelings.

I shall end this chapter by referring to Winnicott's paper interestingly entitled 'Hate in the Countertransference', written in 1947. In describing an analyst's work, in particular with psychotic patients, he writes, 'however much he loves his patients he cannot avoid hating them and fearing them, and the better he knows this the less will hate and fear be the motives determining what he does to his patients' (Winnicott 1992, p.195). Through normalising this apparently negative emotion, Winnicott allows us to consider and acknowledge its existence, suggesting that working with his kind of difficulty brings about 'quite a different type of strain'. A patient such as this 'can only appreciate in the analyst what he himself is capable of feeling', and suggests that, as therapists, if we have not addressed certain aspects of our own psyche, then a patient's progress will be inhibited. Hate is a feeling which as Winnicott tells us is a useful part of an analyst's response. And making the analogy with a mother who hates as well as loves her baby tells us that 'the analyst's hate is actually sought by the patient'. Hate is part of a baby's repertoire and one that is particularly necessary when in the process of separation. In using the analogy of the dependent infant, Winnicott makes a parallel between a mother's responses to her child and an 'analyst's hatred of the regressed, needy, and psychotic patient' (Abram 1996, p.172). Winnicott is advocating that by allowing hate and love to live alongside each other then, in the case of the infant's development, a state of ambivalence can ultimately be reached and he links this to an infant's arrival at the stage of concern. For the psychotic patient, whose early environmental failure has caused deficiency or distortion, 'the analyst has to be the first in the patient's life to supply certain environmental essentials' (Winnicott 1992, p.198). In a therapeutic setting this would be such elements as the couch, warmth and comfort, all aspects that are symbolic of a mother's love. For the psychotic patient these elements are not symbolic but actual and, as Winnicott describes, '*are* the analyst's physical expression of love. The couch *is* the analyst's lap or womb'. The intense quality of neediness that a patient such as this expresses place a particular kind of strain upon the analyst and is to 'do with the effort required for an analyst to keep his hate latent'. And the only way to do this is by being aware of its existence. The quality of transference in this kind of work means that the patient will see the analyst 'as he feels himself to be' (Winnicott 1992, p.199).

## Martha

Martha had been adopted at the age of two after an abusive early life. She entered therapy at the age of seven when she suddenly and tragically lost her adopted father. Initially, Martha was both unable and unwilling to communicate verbally and would spend much time either hiding or hitting specific instruments with such force that nothing could be heard above her sound. Attempting to make any verbal connection, such as ordinary 'hallos' and 'goodbyes', proved to be impossible. In fact words in general appeared to be experienced by Martha as persecutory in nature, causing her on occasions to put her fingers in her ears. In one session, and after I had got it horribly wrong, Martha left the music therapy room and then the building. Following her into the garden, she picked up some stones and began to throw them at me. Fearing for my safety, I was forced to call for her mother. Between us we were able to bring Martha back from her persecuted state of mind and into a calmer and more reflective place. It appeared that my words had literally pierced her skin, causing Martha to defend herself against the pain. From that moment onwards in therapy I became intensely aware of my own underlying fear as I entered into our weekly therapeutic sessions. Every week it was necessary that I become mindful of my feelings. If I was not able to keep watch on my own state of mind, I realised that it would take over, preventing authentic connections between Martha and me to take place. The strain of working with Martha was great, but seven years down the line things between us had been able to move on. When appropriate, she was now able to have a conversation, which sometimes included her suggesting different ways of playing together. She began to bring her own ideas to the session and, although it remained precarious at times, we managed to sustain a meaningful relationship.

An infant's early need for his mother is ruthless and evokes a mother's hate. Winnicott implied that the psychotic patient, who is not aware of his own hate, too becomes ruthless in his need for the analyst. And in one of the points in Winnicott's list in why a mother hates her baby there is one which has particular resonance in my work with Martha. He writes, 'he tries to hurt her, periodically bites her, all in love' and 'he shows disillusionment about her. He is suspicious, refuses her good food, and makes her doubt herself, but eats well with his aunt. If she fails him at the start she knows he will pay her out for ever' (Winnicott 1992, p.201). Toward the end of Winnicott's paper he writes:

> An analyst has to display all the patience and tolerance and reliability of a mother devoted to her infant; has to recognize the patient's wishes as needs; has to put aside other interests; in order to be available and to be punctual and objective; and has to seem to want to give what is really only given because of the patient's needs. (1992, pp.202–3)

In summary it is the quality of therapist's presence and what this comes to mean to the patient that is important. Inevitably the therapist's experience will be coloured by the transference and countertransference phenomena which evolve. But this is helpful information for understanding a patient's inner world. Bollas's words in which he reflects upon questions raised by Margaret Little, explain that 'each analyst at any moment should be asking how she is feeling, why she is feeling this, and why now' (1991 p.2). These questions are representative of the 'continuous interplay between the patient's transference and the analyst's countertransference'. The theory of projective identification illuminates this process and leads to an understanding of the questions raised. Our projections are what we need our therapist to know.

# CHAPTER 11

# Therapeutic Practice

*Only from this ambience of mutual unknowing could the symbolic discourse which constitutes the analytic* [music therapy] *process and dialogue be discovered.*

(M. Khan 1986, p.132)

Khan's words reflect the place from which all mothers with their babies and all therapists with their patients begin their new and special relationships. Every different connection brings with it its own unique dynamic and, in the particular one we name as therapy, also elements of a complex and often puzzling quality. It is in the nature of our role as therapist to offer a place and a space in which the children and adults coming to music therapy may bring their struggles along with their pain, in the hope that they will be heard and ultimately understood. But, as we all know, this task is not straightforward. Just as there are many different kinds of human beings, so there are as many varied ways in which early experiences may come to be expressed.

Reflecting upon the written words of psychoanalytic literature, Winnicott made the statement that 'they do not seem to tell us all that we want to know' (Winnicott 2008, p.142). I could imagine writing this sentence in my early years of practice. Faced with the complex issues my initial clinical post as music therapist presented, I too was left to wonder if what I had learned had been enough. Winnicott's initial statement leads him further to wonder in more philosophical terms, 'what for instance, are we doing when we are listening to a Beethoven symphony or making a pilgrimage to a picture gallery...or playing tennis?' Coming to the crux of his musing, he then wonders, 'what is a child doing when sitting on the floor playing with toys [or musical instruments], under the aegis of the mother? [music-mother/father]' (p.142). Indeed! But, as ever, answering his own query, Winnicott turns our focus toward what he considers to be the real puzzle. That is, not what are we doing, rather 'where are we (if anywhere at all)?' (p.142). Winnicott's playfulness shines through as we are invited, in common business-speak, to 'think outside the box'! We may assume that part of our therapeutic function is to discover what our patients are doing in our therapeutic environment and that, if we somehow work out what is needed, they will then be on the path to change. Yet Winnicott's question demands that we stop, think and reflect. Characteristic of his ability to discover and hold a third position, he initially refers to our inner and outer worlds. And taking for granted that we understand the nature of these particular concepts, he reiterates that external reality that connects us to object-relating and object-usage and inner psychic reality is 'the personal property of each individual' (p.143). Having redefined the internal and external areas of being, he then draws our attention to the possibility of a third which, as he suggests, will be variable, depending upon the individual's living experiences, rather than those aspects of human development which are inherited. He explains, 'where there is trust and reliability [there] is a potential space...which the child or adult may creatively fill with playing' (p.146). Our task as therapists then is to discover the potential space in which 'the individual child or adult is able to be creative and to use the whole personality' (Winnicott 2008, p.73).

What is it that as music mothers and music fathers we need to provide for our patients in order that we can create a climate conducive to playing? Just as Winnicott continually made links between the early environmental set-up and the analytic setting, I have come to believe that it is in this area of growth where significant elements of therapeutic practice can be found. Throughout his life's work and arising from his detailed study of the early mother–infant relationship, Winnicott perceived that the elements that are central to a healthy start in life are ones that should be replicated within the therapeutic setting. And as Phillips suggests, Winnicott's belief was that therapy is 'first and foremost the provision of a congenial milieu, a "holding environment"' (Phillips 1988, p.11). Having a secure base provides a child or adult with the possibility of experiencing the freedom to move both literally and emotionally and, in so doing, begin to move towards feeling real. As therapists, enabling a patient to reveal themselves to themselves must be foremost, and for Winnicott this process would not arrive through clever interpretations. For, as he suggests, 'the patient's creativity can only be too easily stolen by a therapist who knows too much' (Winnicott 2008, p.76). Or maybe, dare I suggest, by one who plays too much. We must begin as a mother begins with her baby, by creating a place in which a patient can begin to feel secure enough. Winnicott's message is clear: 'Human infants cannot start to *be* except under certain conditions.' (Winnicott 1990, p.43). In the language influenced by the thinking in attachment theory Holmes identifies five elements which go toward forming the parameters of what he names as being a 'secure base'. These are 'consistency, reliability, responsiveness, non-possessive-warmth, firm boundaries' (Holmes 2003, p.4). As the therapeutic relationship progresses, these building blocks he suggests should ideally become internalised 'as a "place" in the psyche to which the patient can turn when troubled' and even after the therapy has concluded (p.4).

One of the most natural conditions is the boundary which we create around the therapeutic space and in which our patients spend their time with us. Not only does this mark the difference between the enclosed world of therapy and the external world of our patients, but it also establishes a sense of a psychological inside and an external outside.

Part of the way in which the therapeutic boundary functions is to create a space formed through time, initially in the concrete sense. This is defined by such actions as the set time at which a session takes place, the actual length of each session, breaks and, of course, the ending. But, as Winnicott explained, there is also a kind of time which is psychologically based and which allows a child or adult to have a sense that that there is also a place for them in the mind of the therapist. By meeting regularly and consistently, as music mother I create an atmosphere in which the musical relationship we have begun to create can begin to lodge itself in the mind of the patient. Just as they become held in my mind and thought about both in and outside of our real time together, so the music of our relationship starts to find its place within the mind of the child or adult who comes to play. The internal space is matched by the external space in which all the notes, sounds and musical expressions are contained.

Given the nature of the music therapy environment and the attractiveness of the various musical instruments, children and adults usually feel compelled to use them in some way. If we allow our patients to explore freely, then we also give them permission to be spontaneous. But, as Winnicott wrote, 'spontaneity only makes sense in a controlled setting. Content is of no meaning without form' (Davis and Wallbridge 1981, p.140). Form gives shape and brings sense to what happens in therapy. The ways in which we organise the therapeutic space provide a particular environmental shape for our patients. As Winnicott tells us, 'what we do is arrange a professional setting made up of time and a space and behaviour, which frames a limited area of child or child care experience, and see what happens' (Davis and Wallbridge 1981, p.140).

Seeing what happens brings us back to the start of this chapter, that when we begin our new relationship, we are in the area of the unknown, but also one of potential creativity.

Creating shape around a child or adult's musical expressions helps to frame the range of complex feelings that may arise. The nature of music with all its particular elements contains a natural potential for form and is a medium that relates to our more general need for structure, shape and pattern in our daily living. Just consider the elements involved in being able to move for example. If however, our early life experiences have been one of chaos or fragmentation and, as Winnicott considers, before we have 'got an idea of a framework as part of [our] own nature?' (1971, p.228) then the relational patterns and shapes we organise for ourselves in the world will reflect aspects of these early-disjointed experiences. A child whose experience of boundaries has been one of unpredictability or rigidity, can become disabled in his emotional development. As a result, his capacity for feeling free may be inhibited, leaving him to feel anxious.

# Luke

Luke was a bright active nine-year-old who had recently lost his mother to cancer. Father was worried that he was finding things difficult and had noted that Luke had become aggressive toward other members of his family as well as the children in his class at school. The family culture had been one in which boundaries had been quite rigid and therefore left no room for flexibility or free expression. Father's own way of coping with his wife's death was to 'carry on' with a determination not to break down in front of his children. When Luke began his music therapy, he found difficulty in remaining in the room. Initially his feelings would be expressed in a physical manner, by running at fast speed from one side of the room to the other, hitting each wall as he reached it. Following these physical explosions, it became possible on occasions to engage in some musical play together, but only for a short while. After our musical connection, which was usually directed by Luke, once again he would become overcome by his anxious feelings. In order to relieve the intensity of their impact, this time he would open the therapy door, saying he was very hot. Sometimes, and on some pretext, he would actually go outside whilst I would emphasise the boundary of the therapeutic space. It seemed that Luke's rigid family boundaries had disabled Luke's capacity for forming an internal container. Experiencing such a rupture to his life as his mother's death had prompted an internal crisis in which Luke's feelings could no longer be contained. All he felt he could do was to literally try to get away. And Winnicott puts this difficulty so beautifully when he writes, 'the child whose home fails to give a feeling of security looks outside his home for the four walls; he seeks an external stability without which he may go mad' (1971, p.228).

The particular kind of boundary required in order that a child may feel secure is one which is necessary in the therapeutic setting. A therapist who gives a child or adult permission to use the therapeutic setting as they wish, and is able to hold the setting, enables his patient to find their own way of discovering themselves. In psychoanalysis the exploration of the self occurs through the free associations a patient makes whilst lying on the couch. In music therapy, improvisation is the medium that facilitates a child or adult's capacity for exploring themselves along with the therapeutic relationship. Winnicott himself used a form of improvisation in his squiggle game. Like the music therapist who invites a child or adult to play, so in Winnicott's game he would begin by inviting a child to complete a squiggle he had made. Drawing together, a child would eventually offer 'a sample of their internal world' (Phillips 1988, p.15). This particular game, as Phillips describes, has the quality of 'reciprocal free-association', suggesting an unpredictable but creative quality to the exchanges (p.15). It is a game without rules. Yet the squiggle game, like musical improvisation, is play that occurs within a particular frame. And this particular kind of boundary was one which as Davis and Wallbridge explain, was central to all departments of Winnicott's life and present even in the size of paper he chose to use for his squiggle game.

Once a boundary is established within the therapeutic setting, it can become possible for a child or adult to begin to explore the musical environment which, as I have described, usually includes creating music in the moment. Winnicott takes this further by considering the content within a framework and, in his case, the difference between scribbling and creating a picture. In his description of a five-year-old boy who is drawing, Winnicott refers to the fact that when a child scribbles and makes a mess this is not a picture. Rather, this form of expression is one of 'primitive pleasures' arising out of a need to express something of ourselves. If on the other hand a child is able to create a picture, then 'he has found a series of controls that satisfy him' (Davis and Wallbridge 1981, p.139). Perhaps it is possible to see an infant's early vocal and physical expressions as being a form of mess, primitive expressions, which through a mother's continual responses are gradually made meaningful.

Musical improvisation, one could argue, is the freedom to make a 'musical mess'. And it would seem to me that this is an important step in the process of supporting a patient to discover themselves. For 'the person we are trying to help needs a new experience in a specialised setting' and this experience should be 'one of a non-purposive state' (Winnicott 2008, p.74). Being in this non-purposive state allows a child or an adult to communicate a series of 'ideas, thoughts, impulses, sensations' (p.74) which may appear not to be linked and are delivered in their own particular time. As part of this process, one could say that timing is everything, as any kind of interruption may only serve our own needs as therapists, which is to be of help. Bollas writes about the urge in an analyst to question or make a statement, which if badly timed, can be experienced by the patient as an intrusion. An interpretation made at the wrong time can, as he tells us, interrupt the experiencing of 'an important self state that lay dormant' (1991, p.262). Winnicott's concept of holding, or creation of a boundary as described in Chapter 4, stresses the importance of managing experiences, such as the '*completion* (and therefore the *non-completion*) of processes...[that] take place in a complex psychological field' (Davis and Wallbridge 1981, p.98). Verbal or musical interruptions, or other inappropriate interventions, can break into the therapeutic process and can, as Winnicott describes, freeze a situation. An example of this occurred with my patient Tim in Chapter 6. Following my question, Tim had clearly felt that his experience of who he was being at the time, his inner experience of himself, had been interrupted, and vividly expressed its effect upon him through the musical dynamics of his reply.

However, as well as being an aspect of the therapeutic relationship which can become invasive, the timing of a musical intervention can also be exquisite. We can create a musical fit.

## Jane and baby Thomas

In music therapy with baby Thomas and his mother, we begin our time together by establishing the opening boundary, created by our regular 'hallo song'. We sit together on the floor and, holding Thomas facing toward her, I begin to sing to Jane and Thomas. At times I have found that it is not always appropriate to begin with this kind of musical intervention, as quite often a child or adult needs to discover their own way of beginning. With Jane and Thomas, however, this song provided a way for us all to feel that we had arrived. During our music, Jane appeared awkward and looking around the room, found it difficult to engage with her son. It also becomes clear that Thomas could not sustain eye contact with his mother and when Jane tried to catch his gaze he moved his head from side to side. As the music continued, I noticed that Jane was beginning to gently sway in time to the song. Feeling this movement in his mother's body, Thomas shifted his gaze from the lights in the ceiling to the face of his mother. Jane smiled in response, and visibly began to relax. In turn, Thomas fixed his gaze upon his mother's face, drinking her in.

Discovering their own individual moment in which they could find each other arose through the physicality of the music, which allowed mother and Thomas to find their own tempo in which they could connect. A music mother/father's part in facilitating this process is crucial. Just as healthy growth is 'determined by the awareness and empathy of the mother' (Holmes 2003, p.135) healthy progress in therapy requires us to be empathic toward our patients. Empathy, as Holmes describes, occurs when we 'take a small fragment or our own experience and amplify it so that it fits with the person in our charge' (2003, p.4). In musical terms, we tune in. Jane's depression got in the way of her using her ability to tune in to her son, and interrupted her capacity to be empathic. Supporting her, or one could say holding mother in the music, appeared to enable Jane to literally relax into the sounds and become open to the expressions of her son. An empathic state of mind in the carer, whether toward a child or a patient, is one in which an ability to identify and subsequently adapt to the other's needs is promoted. And as Giovacchini tells us, 'the analyst's understanding is based on both emotional receptivity and the knowledge acquitted from clinical experience' (1990, p.75).

Like the mother who uses her own early life experiences to help her with the care of her baby, even unconsciously, so as therapists we can use our personal experiences of pre-verbal life in order to become open to that part of our being which is in our patients. Allowing ourselves to enter into their inner world requires us to 'participate' in their illness, and through the nature of a musical relationship; it is possible for this to happen in a direct way. I am reminded of my earlier reference to Bollas's work with autistic and schizophrenic children, in which he described how the wordless state of the autistic child 'taught him how to attend to this wordless element in the adult' (Bollas 1991, p.3). Opening ourselves to the inner world of our patients, and through the transference and countertransference experiences, Bollas suggests that we will 'partly be preoccupied with the emergence into thought of early memories of being and relating' (1991, p.3). In consequence I believe we will be able to feel with, rather than just about, the autistic child, for example, who is in the room.

Winnicott himself believed that 'the defining characteristic of the analytic setting...was not exclusively verbal exchange' (Philips 1988, p.138). His passionate belief in the continuity rather than differences between 'the vitally important subtle communicating of the infant–mother kind', and 'the child playing and beginning to speak, and the adult talking', led him to make the following statement. That, in analysis, 'the difference between the child and the adult is that the child often plays rather than talks. The difference, however, is almost without significance and indeed some adults draw or play' (Winnicott 1990, p.117). This leads me into the final part of this chapter and brings my discussion almost full circle.

Prompted to discover a way of making sense of what goes on in the therapeutic setting, as I initially explained, I was led to study early development. But, as a primarily non-verbal medium, I was also drawn to consider the role of words within a music therapy relationship. To turn to Winnicott once again:

> What matters to the patient is not the accuracy of the interpretation so much as the willingness of the analyst to help, the analyst's capacity to identify with the patient and so to believe in what is needed and to meet the need as soon as the need is indicated verbally or in non-verbal or pre-verbal language. (Winnicott 1990, p.122)

Winnicott is clearly not denying the function of words as an important aspect of human growth as well as a necessary part of a therapeutic relationship. But his insistence on getting the environment good-enough affirms the qualities of allowing the patient to lead the way. As he tells us, 'psychotherapy [music therapy] is not making clever interpretations; by and large it is a long-term giving the patient back what the patient brings' (Winnicott 2008, p.158). And, referring to the mother's face as a mirror, he tells us, 'I like to think of my work this way, and to think that if I do this well enough the patient will find his or her own self, and will be able to exist and to feel real' (p.158).

I believe it is necessary to find a way in which we can acknowledge and demonstrate our comprehension of what our patients have chosen to reveal, even if our 'word thoughts' may not always be spoken aloud. For a mother with her baby is continuously putting into verbal expressions her thoughts, responses, reflections and understanding of her new baby, even though her infant is yet to acquire the language of words. By doing this she is helping him as well as herself, to manage the everyday fluctuations of daily life. Therefore, at times I believe it is helpful for a child or adult if we acknowledge and clarify their experience, but not when it suits us. As music therapists we are not necessarily schooled in the art of interpretation through words, which I suggest is connected to the already inherent communicative nature of our therapeutic tool. What we learn about is being in a relationship through music and mostly without words. As I have already suggested, there may well be some music therapists for whom being in the music alone is therapy enough. But, in my own clinical experience, there has always come a point with a child or adult when a connection has been made that needs acknowledgement, which if carried out in a good-enough way, can lead to a kind of knowing which may move the therapy on. Arriving at a point in the therapy in which something may be understood, can, as Winnicott tells us, 'carry the therapeutic work forward' (Winnicott 2008, p.68). He is careful to stress that this occurs when there is what he names as being mutual playing, and one which is 'spontaneous, and not compliant or acquiescent' (2008, p.68).

Interpretation, as suggested by Bollas, can behave as a check on our own understanding. Equally, it is also a way of letting a child or adult know that we are thinking about what is going on between us. The challenge comes when what has been communicated is linked to the patient's pre-verbal state of being and therefore is lodged at a time when there were no words. Perhaps it is in this place, in our earliest time of being, that we find an inner music to which we may connect and a language that we can share. For now, I choose to end my book with the words of the person who was always prepared to be himself and, through the music of his words, has taught me a way to think about and speak about my kind of music:

> The searching can come only from the desultory formless functioning, or perhaps from rudimentary playing, as if in a neutral zone. It is only here, in this unintegrated state of the personality that that which we describe as creative can appear. This if reflected back, *but only if reflected back*, becomes part of the organised individual personality, and eventually this is in summation makes the individual to be, to be found; and eventually enables himself or herself to postulate the existence of the self. (Winnicott 2008, p.86)

# References

Abram, J. (1996) *The Language of Winnicott: A Dictionary of Winnicott's Use of Words.* London, UK: Karnac.

Baradon, T., Broughton, C., Gibbs, I., James, J., Joyce, A. and Woodhead, J. (2006) *The Practice of Psychoanalytic Parent–Infant Psychotherapy.* London, UK and New York, NY: Routledge.

Bion, W. R. (1967) *Second Thoughts: Selected Papers on Psycho-Analysis.* London, UK: Heinemann.

Bollas, C. (1991) *The Shadow of the Unthought Known.* London, UK: Free Association Books.

Bollas, C. (1993) *Being: A Character Psychoanalysis and Self Experience.* London, UK: Routledge.

Brown, D. and Pedder, J. (1991) *Introduction to Psychotherapy.* London, UK: Routledge.

MacDonald, A.M. (ed) (1979) *Chambers Twentieth Century Dictionary.* Edinburgh, UK: W&R Chambers Ltd.

Cox, M. (1978) *Structuring the Therapeutic Process: Compromise with Chaos – the Therapist's Response to the Individual and the Group.* Oxford, UK: Pergamon Press.

Bowlby, J., Figlio, K. and Young, R. (1986) *An Interview with John Bowlby on the Origins and Reception of His Work.* London, UK: Free Association Books.

Davis, M. and Wallbridge, D. (1981) *Boundary and Space: An Introduction to the Work of D. W. Winnicott.* London, UK: Karnac.

Douglas, H. (2007) *Containment and Reciprocity: Integrating Psychoanalytic Theory and Child Development Research for Work with Children.* London, UK: Routledge.

Gerhardt, S. (2004) *Why Love Matters.* New York, NY: Brunner-Routledge.

Gibran, K. (1980) *The Prophet.* London, UK: Pan Books.

Giovacchini, P. (ed.) (1990) *Tactics and Techniques in Psychoanalytic Therapy: iii: The Implications of Winnicott's Contributions.* Northvale, NJ: J. Aronson.

Gomez, L. (1997/1998) *An Introduction to Object Relations.* London, UK: Free Association Books.

Greenson, R. R. (1965) 'The working alliance and the transference neurosis.' *Psychoanalytic Quarterly* 34, 155–181.

Grosskurth, P. (1986) *Melanie Klein: Her World and Her Work.* London, UK: Hodder and Stoughton.

Heimann, P. (1950) 'On countertransference.' *International Journal of Psychoanalysis 31*, 81–84.

Hinshelwood, R. D. (2002) 'Countertransference.' In R. Michels, L. Abensour, C. L. Eizirik and R. Rusbridger (eds) *International Journal of Psychoanalysis*. Key Papers Series. London, UK: Karnac.

Hinshelwood, R. D. (1991) *A Dictionary of Kleinian Thought*, 2nd edn. London, UK: Free Association Books.

Holmes, J. (2003) *The Search for the Secure Base*. New York, NY: Brunner-Routledge.

Issroff, J. (2005) *Donald Winnicott and John Bowlby: Personal and Professional Perspectives* with contributions from C. Reeves and B. Hauptman. London, UK: Karnac.

Joseph, B. (1985) 'Transference: The Total Situation.' In E. Bott Spillus (ed.) *Melanie Klein Today, vol. 2, Mainly Practice*. London, UK: Routledge.

Khan, M.M.R. (1986) *The Privacy of the Self, Papers on Psychoanalytic Theory and Technique*. London, UK: Hogarth Press and The Institute of Psycho-Analysis.

Kahr, B. (1996) *D. W. Winnicott: A Biographical Portrait*. London, UK: Karnac.

Karen, R. (1994) *Becoming Attached: First Relationships and How They Shape Our Capacity to Love*. Oxford, UK: Oxford University Press.

Maiello, M. (2004) *Music Therapy for Premature and Newborn Infants*. Gilsum, NH: Barcelona Publishers.

Maiello, S. (1995) 'The sound-object: A hypothesis about prenatal auditory experience and memory' *Journal of Child Psychotherapy 21*, 23–41.

Marrone, M. (1998) *Attachment and Interaction*. London, UK: Jessica Kingsley Publishers.

Meltzer, D. (1976/1994) 'Temperature and Distance as Technical Dimensions of Interpretation.' In A. Hahn (ed.) *Sincerity and Other Works. Collected Papers of Donald Meltzer*. London, UK: Karnac.

Money-Kyrle, R. (1989) 'Normal counter-transference and some of its deviations' in E.B. Spillius, ed. *Melanie Klein Today. Developments in Theory and Practice. Volume 2: Mainly Practice. (The New Library of Psychoanalysis)*. London, UK/New York, NY: Brunner-Routledge.

Naumann, M. (2013) *Information about the Barenboim-Said Academy. Berlin, Germany: Barenboim-Said Academy*. Available online at www.daniel-barenboim-stiftung.org/fileadmin/files/Pdf/130913%20BSA%20Brochure%20ENGLISH.pdf, accessed 2 December 2014.

Padel, J. (2001) 'Winnicott's Thinking.' In M. Bertoloni, A. Giannakoulas, and M. Hermandez, with A. Molino (eds) *Squiggles and Spaces: Revisiting the Work of D. W. Winnicott, vol. I*. London and Philadelphia: Whurr.

Parkes, C. M. (1995) *Bereavement*. London, UK: Tavistock.

Phillips, A. (1988) *Winnicott*. London, UK: Fontana Press.

Pullen (2010) Personal communication.

Robertson, J. and Robertson, J. (1989) *Separation and the Very Young*. London, UK: Free Association Books.

Schore, A. N. (2001) 'Effects of a secure attachment relationship on right brain development, affect regulation, and infant mental health.' *Infant Mental Health Journal 22*, 7–66.

Solomon, H. M. (2004) 'Self creation and the "as if" personality.' *Journal of Analytical Psychology 43*, 5, 635–656.

Sontag, S. (1976) *Illness as Metaphor.* New York, NY: Farrar, Straus.

Stern, D. N. (2002) *The First Relationship: Infant and Mother.* Cambridge, MA: Harvard University Press.

Storr, A. (1991) 'Music in relation to the self.' *Journal of British Music Therapy 5*, 1, 5–13.

Symington, J. (ed.) (2000) *Imprisoned Pain and Its Transformation: A Festschrift for H. Sydney Klein.* London, UK: Karnac.

Winnicott, C., Shepherd, R. and Davis, M. (eds) (1989) *Psychoanalytic Explorations.* London, UK: Karnac.

Winnicott, C., Shepherd, R. and Davis, M. (eds) (1984) *Deprivation and Delinquency.* London, UK: Tavistock.

Winnicott, D. W. (1965) *The Family and Individual Development.* London, UK: Tavistock.

Winnicott, D. W. (1971) *The Child, the Family, and Outside World.* London, UK: Penguin.

Winnicott, D. W. (1984) *Deprivation and Delinquency.* London, UK: Tavistock.

Winnicott. D. W. (1986) *Home Is Where We Start From; Essays by a Psychoanalyst.* London, UK: Penguin.

Winnicott, D. W. (1990) *The Maturational Processes and the Facilitating Environment.* London, UK: Karnac.

Winnicott, D. W. (1992) *Through Paediatrics to Psychoanalysis.* London, UK: Karnac.

Winnicott, D. W. (1988) *Babies and Their Mothers.* London, UK: Free Association Books.

Winnicott. D. W. (1996) *Thinking about Children*, ed. R. Shepherd, J. Johns and H. Taylor Robinson, H. London, UK: Karnac.

Winnicott, D. W. (2008) *Playing and Reality.* London, UK: Routledge.

Winnicott, D. W. and Britton, C. (1944) *The Problem of Homeless Children*, Children's Communities Monograph No. 1.

Woodhead, J. (2004) 'Dialectical process' and 'constructive method': micro-analysis of relational process in an example from parent–infant psychotherapy.' *Journal of Analytical Psychology 49*, 143–160.

Wright, K. (1998) 'Deep calling unto deep: artistic creativity and the maternal object.' *British Journal of Psychotherapy 14*, 4, 453–467.

Wright, K. (1991) *Vision and Separation between Mother and Baby.* London, UK: Free Association Books.

# Subject Index

# Author Index